BETTER PARENTS, BETTER CHILDREN

By Bill C. Marshall

and Christina Mae Marshall

A WORKBOOK FOR A MORE SUCCESSFUL FAMILY IN 21 DAYS.

HAMMOND INCORPORATED
MAPLEWOOD, NEW JERSEY

Acknowledgements

We would like to thank Hugh Baird and Brent Rich for permission to use their book, *Teacher Student Relations* as a guide for construction of the Reality Behavior Training model. We would also like to thank Richard and Kelleen Hemsley for their encouragement and support.

Lastly, we wish to thank our children, Paul, Megan, and Michael for being patient with Mommy and Daddy while we were writing this book.

This book has been developed under the auspices of The Parent-Child Foundation, Atlanta, Georgia.

Editor: Lonye Rasch

Book Design: Lucille Y. Chomowicz

Library of Congress Cataloging in Publication Data

Marshall, Bill C.
    Better parents, better children.
    1. Children — Management — Problems, exercises, etc.
I. Marshall, Christina Mae, joint author.   II. Title.
HQ769.M298   649'.1   78-17691
ISBN 0-8437-3140-0

PREFACE

There are numerous books and articles on the market today about raising children, which are based on research and clinical practice in psychology, psychiatry, social work, and marriage and family counseling. Much of this material is useful, but often it is never put to practical use. In *Better Parents, Better Children*, Bill and Christina Mae Marshall have taken very useful information and presented it in such a way that those who read this book will want to get busy and apply it, and they will know how, as they are shown step-by-step how to become more effective parents.

I have had the opportunity of doing co-therapy with Bill Marshall and have seen few marriage counselors who combine warmth, humor, and wisdom in their counseling as well as Bill does. These are also the virtues that can be learned in *Better Parents, Better Children*. Lesson one deals with learning to communicate with children in a way that makes them feel loved and accepted. Children become much more manageable when they have trust in their parents' love.

Lesson two deals with teaching children to identify and accept the consequences of their actions. In other words, this chapter is written to assist parents in teaching responsibility to their children. In an age where self-gratification has perhaps been taken too far, the instructions in this section bring sanity back into child raising.

Lesson three, which is titled "Reality Behavior Training," contains more material that will assist parents in teaching responsibility to their children. Of special interest to parents who are apprehensive about traditional forms of punishment will be the alternatives offered by the authors.

Kenneth C. Tuttle, Ph.D.

FOREWORD

Dear Parent,

What you have in your hands is a *work*book. It is not a book on childrearing in the conventional sense. Too often parents read books about raising children and have no idea after finishing them how to *use* the information. *Better Parents, Better Children* asks you to do more than simply read. It requires you to become involved actively with its pages, answer questions, fill in blanks, analyze situations, and act out conversations. When you finish working your way through this manual, you will know *how to use* the three techniques it presents.*

This is not a scholarly text or a popular commentary. It is not a discussion of the latest parenting fad or a collection of entertaining case studies. The techniques taught in *Better Parents, Better Children* are ones we have seen change lives and strengthen families. We hope you will give them a chance to improve the quality of your family life.

* We have provided an extra set of the exercises that appear throughout the manual so that both parents may take the tests individually. The duplicate set begins on page 113.

TABLE OF CONTENTS

INTRODUCTION

John has backed his younger brother David into a corner of their room. David won't let John play with his Six Million Dollar Man. He clutches the toy as John threatens to hit him with a hammer if he doesn't let him have the bionic man.

Mom rushes in and grabs the hammer, just as John raises it high over his head. She yanks it out of his little hand with a loud cry and yells at John to go to his room. John glares at her. Again Mom commands John to go to his room and he begins to move. As he passes David, John kicks him. Enraged, Mom swings her palms, striking John's bottom with a loud crack! John begins wailing and runs to his room.

As Mom strokes David's hair, she thinks, "Well, it's happened again. Why should today be different from every other day?" She sees no way out as she joins her child in tears.

Have you been through this? Hundreds of parents are caught in this vicious cycle every day in our society. What would you give to put an end to this kind of scene in your home? Would it be worth a few hours of your time over a three-week period to learn something that might keep you from feeling that rage or fear or sadness?

Somewhere, some parent may find it hard to identify with the preceding anecdote. The vast majority of us, however, finds it all too familiar. As parents, we need all the help we can get.

Parenting Has Never Been Easy

Parenting has been compared to straddling two galloping wild horses at the same time and juggling three containers of nitroglycerine at night . . . in a hurricane! While parenting may not be that difficult, at times it certainly can be a very frustrating and discouraging venture.

The story of Cain and Abel tells us that, from the beginning, children have been a cause of worry, concern and, at times, deep sorrow to their parents. Being a parent is no easier today than it was in the past and, in some ways, it is far more difficult. The well-defined roles of father, mother, and child no longer exist to outline for us how to relate to each other.

Changing sex mores, women's liberation, children's rights movements, the increase of alcoholism, educational innovations in the public schools, drug abuse and the social use of drugs, the decline of organized religion as a social force, and hundreds of new conflicting psychological theories all play havoc with any preset notions we may have had about right and wrong, good and bad. Most adults today are somewhat confused and, as a result, parental discipline can no longer be based on the idea that parents have all the answers. What can a parent do?

The only training most people receive in parenting is what they learn through experiences with their own parents. Your mother and father may have been excellent parents and you probably love them and respect their opinions. But the world they raised you in is very different from the world you are raising your children in. What worked for your mother and father may not be right for you. Many of you are single parents raising a child alone. Many of you are working mothers, traveling fathers or simply people who have varied interests outside the home. Today the home is not the hub of activity it once was.

For a number of reasons parents spend less time with their children. Therefore, it is important that the time they do spend be quality time. For example, in the past if a mother spent a total of three hours a day disciplining and punishing her children, that time was balanced by the other six or seven hours she spent either at peace with them or involved pleasantly in play. Today's working mother may only have a total of three hours a day with her children.

The Three R's of Parenting:
Relationship
Responsibility
Reality

This manual contains three lessons, each teaching a basic and effective principle for dealing with children. Each lesson expands on one of the three R's of good parenting.

Relationship

Lesson one will teach you how to use a tool called Reflective Communication. You will learn how to communicate with your child by reflecting his feelings and thoughts, thereby developing a more loving relationship with him.

Today the most important thing you can have going for you as a parent is an open, trusting relationship with your children. This kind of relationship allows you to guide firmly and to enforce rules with a minimum of resentment and a maximum of cooperation. It makes it easier for both you and your child to say the words we all find hard to say: "I made a mistake"; "That was my fault"; "I apologize"; "I'm sorry."

Communication is the key. Your children face the same confusing world you do. They need to be able to talk with you. Opening the lines of communication is the first step you must take before you can employ any other theory or principle of parenting. Non-directive counseling, directive counseling, transactional analysis, reality therapy, and psychotherapy all must await the establishment of communication between parent and child. *Relationship*, the first "R" of parenting, is established through Reflective Communication.

Responsibility

Lesson two will teach you to use the predictable consequences of your child's own actions as an alternative to punishment. Your child will learn that his actions have consequences for which he is responsible, consequences he must endure if he persists in certain behaviors.

Reality

The third lesson deals with Reality Behavior Training (RBT), a problem-solving technique that helps your child deal with life as it really is, not as he would like it to be. RBT provides an effective outline for you and your child to follow as you confront and solve problems together.

How to Use this Manual

1. Plan on spending one week on each lesson. If you complete a lesson in less than seven days, spend the rest of the week reviewing and practicing what you have learned. In 21 days you will be well on your way to becoming a better parent with better children.

2. Consider the benefits of inviting some of your friends to form a study group with you. Your group could meet several times each week to work through the manual together. Or you could meet only once a week and simply compare test results or discuss the material. You are likely to find that you learn even more from the manual if you know that friends have set aside a time to meet with you to discuss the book and are expecting you to be prepared to contribute something to the discussion.

A Word Before You Begin

People tend to be skeptical of anything they do not understand fully. You may be wondering right now if this course can really do anything to make you a better parent. It may be hard for you to believe you can improve on skills you feel ought to come naturally.

As you study the course, we have no doubt that many of the principles will have a familiar ring. You will find that, in some way, you have attempted to use these ideas in the past. What the workbook will do for you is to give a definite form, direction, and name to your own good common sense. The course will give you needed confidence as it assures you that your instincts are correct.

The techniques taught in *Better Parents, Better Children* have proven effective for thousands of families across the country. They can work for you, too. However, as you study, please remember that no *one* technique can be applied universally. There is no panacea for the ills of human relationships. Different situations and personalities require different solutions. Use the methods you are about to learn flexibly and interchangeably. Remember, too, that sometimes a pat, a hug or a kiss is all a child really needs.

If you fail the first few times you attempt these techniques, *do not try harder*. Just go back and learn the concepts better. Remember also that practice makes perfect.

LESSON ONE:
REFLECTIVE COMMUNICATION

A Relationship Builder

Pretest

This pretest will gauge how much you know about reflective communication now. At the end of the lesson, you will take the test again; compare your two sets of responses, and see how much you have learned.

As you take the pretest, please answer truthfully. You are the only one who need see your replies and there is nothing to be gained by responding untruthfully.

Under each child's statement, write how you would normally respond:

Example: 1. CHILD: I surely had a good time at the ball game.
                  RESPONSE: I am glad you had a nice time.

2. Look, Dad! I cleaned up my room all by myself.

3. Dad, will you stay with me for a little while before I go to sleep?

4. Susy has such beautiful hair. I try and try to make mine look better, but it doesn't.

5. You're the best Mom in the whole world.

6. I shouldn't have hit Tommy. It was wrong.

7. But, Mom, I don't want my hair in a ponytail. It's my hair anyway.

8. Dad, is this model right? Is it good enough?

9. I want to call Evelyn for a date but . . .

10. My teachers never give me a chance. They seem to get angry at me for no reason at all.

11. I want to button my own coat. I'm big now.

12. Dad, I don't want to make this decision. You make it instead.

13. I don't think I'll ever get over Bill. How could he ever drop me for that Susan Chalmers?

14. Everybody else gets to go to the city alone. You just don't trust me.

15. I surely am glad that you and Dad love me enough to set rules for me. Jody's parents don't and she wishes they did.

16. Mom, you are always telling me what to do.

17. If I want to stay out late, you can't stop me.

18. You didn't treat Janet like this when she was my age.

19. You never listen to me.

20. What I do is my business, not yours.

Reflective Communication: The Beginning of Constructive Dialogue

People want to communicate their thoughts, opinions, experiences, and feelings; they want to be understood. This is especially true of parents and children. Although children want to talk to their parents and their parents want to talk to them, often the right kind of conversation never materializes.

Conversation must allow the child to express opinions and feelings without fear of ridicule. Love, concern, and understanding should be communicated, even if approval of the child's behavior is not. Reflective communication will get the ball rolling toward the right kind of conversation in your home.

What Is Reflective Communication?

Reflective communication is a method of reflecting back to your child his emotions and thoughts in such a way that he knows you care about him and his problems. By using reflective communication you build a warm, trusting relationship with your child. From this jump-off point, many behavior problems can be solved without anger or hurt feelings.

Reflective communication will:

1. Help you understand your child better

2. Help your child see that you are interested, you are listening, and you understand

3. Help you initiate conversations that will build a positive relationship and effectively communicate your love and concern for your child

4. Help you talk, rather than fight when your child is upset

5. Help your child identify and define specific feelings so that he can recognize, accept, and deal with intense emotions in a positive way.

Now that is quite a lot for one parenting tool to do, but it works! As you study and practice reflective communication, you will be pleasantly surprised to find how well you can use it and how effective it can be in your own family.

Reflective communication has another important effect on your relationship with your children. It gives you greater influence with them. *Parents seem to agree that they would rather influence their children than coerce them.* But, until a child feels understood, he cannot be influenced. Unless he thinks you understand what he is saying, your advice or instructions do not really relate to his particular situation.

Think for a moment. Your child is sick. You have just called the doctor for advice. Before you describe the symptoms, your doctor prescribes a drug for your child. Obviously you will not put much stock in the doctor's advice because it was not based on an understanding of the problem.

Your child can react the same way when you advise or instruct him before he feels you know what you're talking about. You may understand what the child is saying, your advice may be excellent, but unless the child feels that you understand he will not be influenced. Reflective communication helps your child see that you have listened to him and you do understand.

You will find that reflective communication is not some mysterious psychological technique, hard to comprehend and difficult to use. Actually it is quite simple. Basically it involves reflecting back to the child the emotion or the thought he has just communicated to you. At the same time, you avoid lecturing or judging his thoughts or feelings.

Employing reflective communication requires two basic skills, which you are about to learn:

1. Listening to your child's thoughts and feelings
2. Making responses that reflect the thoughts and feelings you heard your child express

The key to reflective communication is to respond to your child in a simple, direct way. If he expresses a feeling, then reflect that. If he expresses a thought, then reflect that thought.

Here is an example:

Kurt is 14. He is doing his homework at the kitchen table as his mother is finishing the dishes.

KURT: I hate geometry. It's so dumb. I wish I didn't have to take it.
MOM: You really don't like that subject, huh?
KURT: I certainly don't. Well, I guess I better hit the dumb old geometry books again.

Simple? Yes. Still, children appreciate the understanding expressed by the parent who simply reflects what the child himself openly stated. At some later time it might be appropriate to discuss with Kurt the reasons for having geometry in the curriculum or to lecture him on the importance of receiving good grades, regardless of whether he enjoys the subject or not. Kurt knows that wishing will not make geometry disappear. He only needed to vent a little steam. Mom reflected Kurt's feeling of dislike for geometry and Kurt continued with his homework.

Here is another example:

Dad is reading the paper and his four-year-old Timmy wanders in moodily. Timmy has a towel tied around his shoulders. Superman is his current idol and so he wants to imitate him.

TIMMY: Faster than a speeding bullet (whoosh), able to leap tall buildings in a single bound (boing). I keep jumping Daddy, but I don't fly. Flying would be fun. I wish I could fly like Superman.
DAD: It would be fun to fly, wouldn't it?

Dad could have jumped right in with a judgement on Timmy's thought. "That's silly, son," he could have said. "Superman's only make-believe. People can't really fly." Instead, he reflected the thought that flying would be fun. This kind of response need not necessarily end the conversation. It could be the introduction to a longer talk between parent and child. What the reflective response says to your child is, "I'm listening to you, I hear what you are saying; I'm interested and I care." In this kind of atmosphere your children will trust you enough to discuss their feelings and thoughts at greater lengths and give you your best shot at influencing their lives.

Learning
Reflective
Communication

The skill is learned by practicing its component parts, step-by-step. This workbook will challenge you to read through various dialogues, alternately assuming the role of parent, then child in order to gain insight into your child's point of view. You will complete written exercises, test yourself, and try new skills in real life. When you have completed the lesson, you will take a post-test, exactly like the pretest. By comparing your pre- and post-test answers, you will be able to see how much you have learned.

As you try to reflect your children's thoughts and feelings, remember the following guidelines:

1. **Don't simply parrot what the child has said.** For example,
CHILD: "I'm angry."
PARENT: "You feel angry."
If at all possible, use synonyms: "I'm angry"; "You feel irritated"; or "This has really irritated you." Synonyms convey the same message and yet keep you from repeating verbatim what the child just said.

2. **Make your reflective responses shorter than the child's statement.** As a parent you should try to condense the child's message to its most vital meaning. A child's 10-minute tirade about how terrible his former best friend is might be condensed to, "Tommy has really hurt your feelings." Of course, this is assuming that you have perceived that hurt feelings are behind the child's angry words. If you know, for example, that Tommy has made a new friend and is currently spending more time with him than with your child, then this is a feeling response that is likely to hit home. If the child is just momentarily upset by some prank the other child has played, you might respond to the tirade with, "Tommy has really made you angry." Such a response is far more calming to an upset child than yelling at him to simmer down.

3. **Don't be afraid to try.** As you attempt to respond to your child in terms of his feelings, to condense his messages to their essence, and to slice incisively to the core of his emotions, you may miss the mark completely! In spite of this possibility, please don't be afraid to attempt a feeling response. If you are wrong and the emotion you reflect is not at all what your child is feeling, your child will correct you. More important, your child will know that you are trying to understand and that you want to share his joys and sorrows. If you are correct in the feelings you reflect, your child will know that you understand and will want to share even more with you. Either way you win!

Dealing
with
Feelings

The major difficulty in dealing with feelings is that sometimes people don't say what they mean. At times feeling reflection involves perceiving a feeling not openly stated by the child and reflecting it back to him. To do this, the parent must slice through what the child seems to be saying and get at what he is really saying. The child who is acting very angry may actually be hurt or frustrated. The child who belligerently refuses to do something may be frightened. The child who is boastful and obnoxious may feel insecure or inadequate.

Here is a real-life situation that we observed. Read through this dialogue with your spouse or a friend. Take turns being the two people. Try to remember times you have been in situations like this as a parent or as a child. Try to feel that way again as you say the words.

TEEN:	Susan Pate thinks she's so neat. Who does she think she is anyway? Farah Fawcett Majors—with that wild hair style and her tight jeans? She makes me sick . . . that dumb voice and those batting eyelashes. If that's the kind of girl boys like, then they're all dumb too.
PARENT:	Pretty wild girl, huh?
TEEN:	You said it.
PARENT:	Dresses kind of flashy.
TEEN:	I would call a T-shirt with "I was made to be loved" printed on it flashy, yes.
PARENT:	You feel a little bit jealous of Susan?
TEEN:	Jealous! How can you say such a thing? Jealous of that shallow, stupid, flipped out . . .
PARENT:	Whoa, sweetheart. We can be jealous of people we don't admire or like or want to be like. We're still a little jealous anyway. It's not a rational thing. It's just human.
TEEN:	She's everything I really despise. It doesn't make sense. She really is . . . and yet sometimes I can't help but wonder what it would be like to have all that hair, all those clothes, all those boys. But it just doesn't make sense. I despise her and yet . . .
PARENT:	Our emotions can be so confusing sometimes.
TEEN:	They sure can.

How do you feel after living this experience from both points of view? In this example, the parent used both levels of feeling response. First, the parent made the insightful statement that perhaps the daughter felt jealous. The more obvious feelings were disgust and anger, but the parent looked beyond these. Later, by saying that emotions can be confusing, the parent simply reflected to the daughter her statement that things didn't make sense. Jealousy can be a gnawing burden to bear. What a relief to discuss it openly and know that Mom or Dad understands!

Feelings are Basic

Because feelings are more basic than thoughts, they convey a more accurate picture of what is going on inside people. It is from feelings that thoughts and actions emerge. The process may go something like this:

1. I feel angry so I don't like you.
2. I don't like you so I will hit you.

BETTER PARENTS, BETTER CHILDREN

Consider the situation where your child has hit another child. As parents, our most natural reaction is to approach the problem first from the standpoint of the hitting. Of course the hitting must be dealt with, but often it can be approached most effectively by way of the emotion that prompted it—the child's anger or hurt or whatever feeling we discern caused the action.

Here are two more parent-child exchanges; two versions of the same situation. Again, take turns playing the roles. Get into it. Believe it.

Tommy, age six, has just popped Mike, age six, on the nose and now they are scuffling on the sidewalk. Tommy's mother rushes from her house and brings Tommy inside.

TOMMY: (bawling) I hate that stupid Mike.

MOM: You stop that yelling, young man. What did you think you were doing? . . . fighting in the street like that . . . making a big scene. How many times have I told you never to hit other children?

TOMMY: He was teasing me.

MOM: I don't care what he was doing. You don't hit other children. Now go upstairs to your room and stay there 'til I tell you to come down.

TOMMY: (still crying) He was teasing me. He kept calling me shorty and freckle face. I told him he better stop it.

MOM: I think I just told you to get upstairs.

TOMMY: I hate Mike. I'm not a shorty.

MOM: You shouldn't hit anyway. Now go upstairs.

TOMMY: I don't like you anymore.

Of course we don't want our children hitting others when they become upset; however, before Mom and Tommy can talk together about the rule that he not hit, Tommy needs to calm down. Reflective communication can have a very calming effect. Read through the same situation using reflective communication:

TOMMY: I hate that stupid Mike.

MOM: You are really angry at Mike.

TOMMY: I'm really mad. Mike was teasing me.

MOM: He was making fun of you.

TOMMY: He kept calling me freckle face and shorty. I told him he better stop it.

MOM: Teasing can make you very angry.

TOMMY: Yeah (quieting down). I told him not to.

MOM: Mike's teasing hurt your feelings.

TOMMY: Yeah (calm now).

After talking about the incident some more, mother can begin to discuss with Tommy why she does not want him to hit and what the consequences will be if he does not stop hitting. The important thing is that because Mom indicated to Tommy by reflective communication that she knows he is angry as well as hurt, Mom and Tommy are talking now instead of fighting.

When you read the part of Tommy, how did you feel at the end of each scene? After reading through the first dialogue, were you ready to listen to Mom about anything? Can you see how important the calming effects of reflective communication can be?

A
Feeling
Vocabulary

Basic to the effective reflection of feelings are

1. the ability to listen
and
2. an adequate "feeling vocabulary."

In order to reflect, you must first listen carefully. Listening is not simply keeping quiet while the other person talks. It requires that you focus your attention on the speaker. You should not be thinking about what your next statement will be. Your attention should be on what the child is saying.

Second, you must begin to think in terms of feelings. It is amazing how hard it is for people to describe a wide variety of feelings. They just don't seem to have the words. Below you will find a list of feeling words that may be useful.

Remember, reflective communication is for everyday use. It does not necessarily mean a big, long scene with your child every time you turn around. A word, a sentence or a lengthy discussion may be effective, depending on the situation. On page 10, you will find the first of several exercises designed to teach you how to do reflective communication. Study hard, think, do the exercises. Do them more than once if you feel you need the extra practice.

Feeling
Vocabulary

afraid	discouraged	happy	love
angry	disgust	hate	proud
anxious	doubtful	helpless	regret
awed	drained	hesitant	resentful
bored	embarrassed	hopeful	revulsion
confused	enjoy	hurt	sad
contempt	envy	inadequate	scared
contented	excited	insecure	shock
cruddy	fear	insincere	sorrow
depressed	frustrated	jealous	timid
despondent	glad	like	uncertain
disappointed	gratitude	lonely	worried

9

Feeling
Vocabulary
Exercise

Please read each of the following statements and write what **feeling** you think the child is most likely experiencing. There may be many correct answers for each statement. Some replies, however, are probably more accurate than others. On page 12 , you will find the one or more feelings considered most accurate.

Example:

Child's Statement	Child's Feeling
Daddy, Daddy, I picked up all my toys.	proud, excited

1. No matter how hard I try, I still can't make friends.

2. Tom is younger than I and he can walk to school by himself.

3. I don't like it when you go and leave me here.

4. Why can't we go to the circus for my birthday?

5. Oh, boy! Only two more days 'til my birthday.

6. There's nothing to do and nobody to play with.

7. I can't do this homework. It's too hard for me.

8. I'll get bigger someday, won't I, Mommy?

9. I did a good job.

10. You never listen to me.

11. Playing the piano is dumb. Who can learn all those notes anyway?

12. But I'm not Jill and I can't be like her because I'm me.

13. I don't care if Jane gets a new dress for the dance. Who wants a new dress anyway?

14. It's nice just to be with you.

15. All the kids laughed at me when I tried to read today. I'll never read again.

16. I didn't mean to do it.

17. I don't want to live your kind of life.

18. You never say anything nice to me.

19. Oh Mom, it was absolutely the grossest movie I've ever seen! It really made me sick. I still feel a little shaky.

20. (Crying): I wish I had never been born.

Answers to Feeling Vocabulary Exercise

1. sad, lonely
2. resentful, hurt, envy
3. scared, insecure, sad
4. disappointed, angry
5. happy, excited
6. bored, lonely
7. frustrated, angry, helpless
8. anxious, hopeful
9. happy, proud
10. angry, frustrated
11. frustrated, discouraged
12. resentful, angry
13. jealous
14. love, happy, contented
15. hurt, discouraged, embarrassed
16. sorrow, regret
17. anger, resentment, contempt, disgust
18. hurt, sorrow
19. shock, revulsion
20. sad, depressed, despondent

How did you do? If you had trouble, study the exercise again. Use the list on page 9 . Look over the answers above. Consider the feeling words and their meanings. Begin to develop your feeling vocabulary. Now please turn to page 13 and complete that exercise.

Feeling Reflection Exercise

You are now ready to formulate some feeling reflections. In this exercise you will be asked to write a reflective response to the child's statement. Write what you perceive the child is feeling, but this time respond in complete sentences. (Hint: You do not always have to use the word "feel" in your replies. If the child says he hates to play the piano and you can tell he is frustrated, your response could be "You're frustrated" or "It can be frustrating at times to learn new music," as well as "You *feel* frustrated.") On page 15 , you will find suggested appropriate responses.

Example:

CHILD: Daddy, Daddy, I picked up all my toys.
RESPONSE: Boy, I'll bet that makes you proud.

1. No matter how hard I try, I still can't make friends.

2. Tom is younger than I and he can walk to school by himself.

3. I don't like it when you go and leave me here.

4. Why can't we go to the circus for my birthday?

5. Oh boy! Only two more days 'til my birthday.

6. There's nothing to do and nobody to play with.

7. I can't do this homework. It's too hard for me.

8. I'll get bigger someday, won't I, Mommy?

9. I did a good job.

10. You never listen to me.

11. Playing the piano is dumb. Who can learn all those notes anyway?

12. But I'm not Jill and I can't be like her because I'm me.

13. I don't care if Jane gets a new dress for the dance. Who wants a new dress anyway?

14. It's nice just to be with you.

15. All the kids laughed at me when I tried to read today. I'll never read again.

16. I didn't mean to do it.

17. I don't want to live your kind of life.

18. You never say anything nice to me.

19. Oh, Mom, it was absolutely the grossest movie I've ever seen! It really made me sick. I still feel a little shaky.

20. (Crying): I wish I had never been born.

Answers to Feeling Reflection Exercise

In this exercise you were asked to write reflective communication responses to 20 statements made by children. As you compare your responses with those below, notice that the child's feelings are always being considered in the reflective response. Remember that there can be more than one feeling expressed. That is why we have included more than one response.

1. It's hard to be lonely.
   You feel sad.

2. You resent the fact that Tom can do something you can't, don't you?
   It hurts your feelings that Tom is trusted more than you.

3. It scared you to be left here.
   You feel worried when we leave you.

4. You're very disappointed.
   You're angry.

5. I'll bet you're really excited.
   That sure makes you happy, doesn't it?

6. It's certainly no fun to be bored.
   It's hard to be lonely.

7. Homework can be frustrating at times.

8. Are you worried about getting bigger?
   You really hope you'll get bigger.

9. Wow, that makes you proud.
   You sound really happy.

10. You are angry at me.
    It's frustrating to think no one is listening.

11. You feel discouraged.
    Trying to make your fingers do the right thing can be very frustrating.

12. You resent being compared to Jill, don't you?
    It makes you angry to be compared to Jill.

13. You seem to be a little jealous of Jane's new dress.
    You're disappointed that you didn't get a new dress, too.

14. I love you, too.
    It's a happy feeling, isn't it?

15. I'll bet it hurt when the kids laughed.
    It made you angry when they laughed at your reading.

16. You feel sorry you did it, huh?
    It makes you sad that this happened, doesn't it?

17. You seem disgusted by the way we live.
    You find our life-style contemptible.
    You seem angry at us.

18. That hurts your feelings.
    It makes you sad when I don't say nice things.

19. You were really revolted by that movie.
    That movie shocked you.

20. You must really be depressed.
    You feel so despondent.

How did you do this time? If you had trouble, study the exercise again. Not everyone is comfortable with feeling words. You may need to practice reciting sentences that reflect feelings until you are comfortable with them. Remember that to any statement, there are several correct feeling responses. The examples given are just that—examples of good reflective communication. You should reflect in a way comfortable for you. Your responses will be good ones if you listen carefully to your child and are sincerely interested in showing him that you have heard what he has said.

Now let's consider some other benefits of feeling reflection.

Benefits of Feeling Reflection

Not only does feeling reflection improve communication, build a loving relationship, and act as an introduction to longer talks, but it has several interesting side effects as well.

Parents who have used feeling reflection conscientiously have found that their children begin to view people and events in terms of feelings too. These children gain a "feeling vocabulary." At early ages they understand the meaning of words like frustrated, hurt, bored, and confused. Because they can label their feelings, they can deal with them more easily. The child who has no word for his feelings may simply sit and cry or whine when a toy proves too advanced for him or a situation overly confusing. The emotionally educated child can tell his parent that he is upset because the situation confuses him or that he doesn't understand what to do with the toy.

A three-year-old who had been given a toy meant for an older child was heard to say, "Mama, I don't know how to do this. It confuses me." He knew that what he was feeling was something called confusion and that that word would immediately tell his parent how he felt. We all know what a relief it can be to tell someone else how we feel and how upsetting it is to find that we just aren't able to communicate. The next time you need to tell someone how you feel, try doing it without using any of the words on page 9 . See if you don't wind up crying or hitting something!

From Understood Child to Understanding Child

Parents who use feeling reflection have also found that eventually their children begin to reciprocate. One mother reported that after she yelled at her children for a very slight offense, one child said with great empathy, "Gee Mom, you're really upset. Has it been a very frustrating day?" The child knew that his mother's outburst was out of proportion to the incident and that there were feelings there that had nothing to do with what the children had done. The question stopped the mother cold. She realized that her day had not been a good one and that she was taking her frustrations out on the children. She apologized for having flown off the handle and the evening proceeded pleasantly.

A child whose parents use feeling reflection will become not only an understood child, but an understanding child.

Thought Reflection

We have been discussing reflective communication in terms of feeling reflection only. You have learned how to use this technique and what results to expect. Now let's talk about thought reflection, another aspect of reflective communication.

Thought reflection is reflecting what the child is thinking:

> CHILD: Mr. Brown is the best teacher I've ever had. He's really fair and he's so interesting to listen to.
>
> PARENT: You think he's a pretty good teacher.

Thought reflection is concerned with facts rather than emotions. When you reflect thought, you reflect opinions the child holds and things he wants to do, to be or to accomplish.

Here are some more examples:

BOY: Dad, I saw this great picture in *Sports Afield* of a bass this man caught in Michigan. It was 20 pounds!

DAD: Wow! That was a real whopper of a fish!

BOY: Jeff is so cool. All the guys like him and the girls fall all over themselves for him.

DAD: Jeff certainly is popular.

GIRL: I'd give anything to make the final cut for cheerleader.

MOM: It would mean a lot to you to be a cheerleader.

GIRL: I just don't see why Kathy gets to stay up later than I do.

DAD: You don't understand why Mom and I make you go to bed earlier than Kathy.

These parents used thought reflection well. If they had responded differently, they may have either brought the talk to a dead end or caused the conversation to become unpleasant, as in these examples:

BOY: Dad, I saw this great picture in *Sports Afield* of a bass this man caught in Michigan. It was 20 pounds.

DAD: That's nice, son.

BOY: Jeff is so cool. All the guys like him and girls fall all over themselves for him:

DAD: Well, I think Jeff's a punk. His hair's too long and his attitude is bad. You are a lot better off not being like him.

GIRL: I'd give anything to make the final cut for cheerleader.

MOM: It won't be the end of the world if you don't make it, Janet. You can try again next year, dear.

GIRL: I just don't see why Kathy gets to stay up later than I do.

DAD: Well, to begin with, she's older than you and besides that she gets up cheerfully every morning and you're a bear even with an extra hour in bed.

Analysis of
Examples

There is nothing wrong with the preceding responses except that they are not heading the conversation in a productive direction. In the first example, father's statement, "That's nice, son," doesn't indicate much interest on Dad's part and is likely to end the conversation right there.

In the second example, Jeff may be every inch an undesirable character. Nevertheless, Pete admires him and wants to be like him. Dad's comment won't change that. It will only make Pete unlikely to talk with his Dad again about his feelings concerning Jeff.

In the third example we can see that, to Janet, being a cheerleader *this year* is important. Mom's response tells Janet her mother doesn't understand at all. Janet is therefore not encouraged to talk to her mother.

In the last example, there is probably going to be a fight over bedtime rules. If father had responded reflectively, the child would have felt encouraged to talk about her opinion that the rule is unfair.

Later in the conversation Mom could discuss the reasons why Kathy gets to stay up later just as Dad in example two could air his views on Jeff later on, and Mom could eventually try to help Janet see that life will go on even if she doesn't become a cheerleader. But these discussions must take place *after* the parent has gathered enough information to make his comments relevant to what the child is thinking. A child will be more willing to listen to a parent when he senses that the parent has made an effort to understand him and knows something about his situation.

Thought reflection communicates the same important messages as feeling reflection: I'm listening; you are worth listening to; I have heard what you said; my advice or instructions are based on an understanding of your particular situation.

Thought
Reflection
Exercise

In this exercise you will be asked to supply a thought reflection in response to the child's statement. Respond in complete sentences and then compare your answers with those on page 22. Remember that your responses need not be exactly like those on page 22, but they should match them in tone and general content.

1. I don't like nursery school.

2. I don't like dogs.

3. Some adults are really crazy.

4. My homeroom teacher is the greatest.

5. I want to be just like you when I grow up.

6. It seems that we always fight around our home. I wish our home was like the Marshall's.

7. Jane got angry at me today. I'll never be her friend again.

8. I'm in the wrong class. This work is too hard for me.

9. Why can't you be more like Jane's mom?

10. I never get to stay up late like John and Bill.

11. Oh, Mom, I wish you understood me.

12. It's none of your business what I do on my dates.

13. You only think of what's good for you and not what is good for me.

14. You don't trust me.

15. Summer school didn't help one bit. I don't understand chemistry any better at all.

16. I'm going to jog every night and eat nothing but grapefruit for two weeks. I've just got to lose 10 pounds.

Answers to Thought Reflection Exercise

1. You don't want to go to school.

2. Dogs aren't your favorite animals.

3. Grownups can really be different at times.

4. Your teacher is pretty sharp.

5. You think I'm a pretty good Dad, huh?

6. The Marshall's have a happier home than we do?

7. You don't want to play with Jane anymore.

8. You think your homework is too difficult for you.

9. You think I should be different from the way I am.

10. You think you should be allowed to stay up later.

11. You don't think I know what you are feeling.

12. You think I'm invading your privacy by asking you questions.

13. You think we don't care about you.

14. You don't think I have much confidence in you.

15. In your opinion it was a waste of time.

16. It's really important to you to lose weight.

How did you do? Remember that your responses need not be identical to these to be right. They need only be along the same general lines.

Reflecting Thoughts *and* Feelings

We have been teaching you reflective communication by dividing it into two parts: *feeling reflection* and *thought reflection*. Our aim was to make learning the concepts easier. The division was *not* made so that you would feel you' must analyze every statement your child makes to decide whether to reflect a *feeling* or a *thought*. Don't become tongue-tied trying to figure out exactly what the very best response would be. Listen to your child and then reflect what you hear. If you hear feelings, reflect them. If you hear thoughts, reflect them. Be natural. Relax. If you care and are trying, your child will know it. Remember that any statement a child makes could warrant either thought or feeling reflection. To the five-year-old who states, "I'd like to smash Brent in the face," you could reply, "You'd really like to hit him" or "You're really angry at Brent" or even "Brent has hurt your feelings, hasn't he?", depending on which you think is true under the circumstances.

See how many kinds of responses could be given in the following situations:

Billy has been told by his father that he cannot go on a hike that his friends are planning and he complains to his mother:

> BILLY: Every guy I know is going on the three-day hike except me. Dad says I'm too young. He thinks it's too dangerous and he won't let me go.

> *Mother could respond:*

> You **think** Dad is being unreasonable.

> or

> You **think** Dad doesn't have much confidence in you.

> or

> It **hurts** your **feelings** to think Dad doesn't believe you can handle it.

> or

> It's kind of **embarrassing** to be the only one not going.

As you can see, both thought and feeling reflection can be appropriate here. Thought reflection and feeling reflection can be used during the same conversation. Because you begin with one does not mean you cannot use the other. There are no hard and fast rules here. The important objective of reflective communication is to listen carefully to your child and then respond in such a way that he knows you are listening and you are trying to understand. You can use reflective communication once during a conversation or many times. Reflect as it feels right to you.

Read through the following situation in which the parent uses reflective communication effectively so that you can experience how it feels. Remember, by playing both parts you get more out of the exercise.

Nine-year-old Jenny is moping around the house, being a general nuisance because her best friend is moving from the neighborhood to a city far away.

> MOM: Jenny, what's the matter with you today? That is the longest face I've ever seen.
> JENNY: Ellen's going to move and I won't have anybody to play with.
> MOM: You'll be lonely without her, won't you dear?
> JENNY: Yes. I don't know what I'll do when she's gone.
> MOM: It will be hard. You're so used to being together.
> JENNY: Yeah. I just don't see why they have to move now.
> MOM: It doesn't seem fair.
> JENNY: It just doesn't seem right. I don't know what I'll do.
> MOM: It's hard when our friends move away.
> JENNY: Yeah . . . Well, guess I'll go outside for a while.

Now let's see what could happen if reflective communication is not used.

MOM: Jenny, what's the matter with you today? That's the longest face I've ever seen.

JENNY: Ellen's going to move and I won't have anybody to play with.

MOM: Don't worry, dear, you'll make new friends quickly enough.

JENNY: But I'm going to miss her so much.

MOM: You'll get over it. People adjust.

JENNY: Oh, Mom (beginning to cry); I'll be so lonely.

MOM: Crying won't help, Jenny. You are a big girl and things like this are part of life. (Jenny continues to cry without saying anything.)

MOM: I'm sorry Ellen's moving, but there is nothing I can do about it. (Jenny's still crying.)

MOM: Why don't you run along and play now? Believe me, crying won't help you. You'll just have to be strong.

As we compare the responses in the two dialogues we see that the second mother told Jenny the truth and gave her perfectly good advice. Jenny *will* get over Ellen's move and she *will* make new friends, but that is not the point. People do adjust and we do have to learn to be strong when there is sadness in our lives, but that's not the point either. *The point is that mother did not listen to Jenny and Jenny is not listening to her.* Jenny feels sad. She wants and needs understanding. Before mother can talk to Jenny about these facts of life, Jenny must know that Mom understands her. Statements of understanding (reflective communication) should precede advice, instruction or probing.

This simply means that your child is more likely to take your advice, carry out your instructions or supply you with information after she sees that you are listening. For example, if your child storms into the house and yells, "I hate school!," your natural reaction is to ask, "Why?," which will probably get you a vague answer like, "I just do, that's all." If instead you reflect, "You are really angry about something. What is it?," your question or probe may get better results. For example, the child may reply, "Mr. Jones gave my paper a C and I worked really hard on it. I thought it was worth at least a B." *Remember,* when children are upset, reflect before you advise, instruct or probe.

Another example will help you see that reflective communication can also be helpful with older children. A 15-year-old girl and her mother, on their way to buy material to make the girl's prom dress, pass a dress shop. The girl stops and stares longingly at a formal displayed in the store's window.

GIRL: That's a gorgeous dress.

MOM: Oh yes, that is beautiful!

GIRL: Kathy Stone shops here all the time, but it's so expensive we couldn't afford anything in here. I guess we better head on down to the fabric store.

MOM: You feel sad that we have to make your prom dress.

GIRL: Oh, I know you'll make me a lovely formal, Mom, but sometimes I can't help but wonder what it would be like to buy clothes from a shop like this.

MOM: Not having a lot of extra money can be depressing at times.

GIRL: Yeah.

MOM: It would be nice to own a dress like that. I'd buy it for you if I could, dear.

GIRL: I know that, Mom. Listen, everyone in town has already seen that dress. The one you'll make me will be a real original, right?

MOM: Right.

GIRL: Okay. Let's quit blabbing and get to the fabric store.

As you can see from this example, reflective communication has a calming effect. It allows parent and child to work through problems and difficult situations rationally and, at the same time, build a more loving relationship.

The same situation could work out quite differently if reflective communication is not used.

GIRL: That's a gorgeous dress.

MOM: No point in mooning over that. It probably costs a fortune.

GIRL: I'm sure it does. Kathy Stone shops here all the time, but it's so expensive we couldn't afford anything in here. I guess we better head on down to the fabric store.

MOM: I should say so, with prices like that. Why, I could make five dresses for the price of that one, I'll bet.

GIRL: I'm sure you can, Mom, but sometimes I get tired of all homemade clothes. I can't help but wonder what it would be like to buy clothes from a shop like this.

MOM: Your clothes are just fine and, believe me, it costs money to outfit a teen-age girl in any kind of clothes. If I were you, I'd be grateful. There are a lot of girls with much less.

GIRL: Well, I don't have any friends with much less.

MOM: Listen here, young lady. Your father works very hard to provide for you and then you say things like that. I think that's terrible.

GIRL: Oh, you don't understand.

In neither instance did the mother buy the dress in the store window. But that is not the point. *The point is that through reflective communication the girl comes to feel her mother is on her side, wanting to understand and to help.* Our teen-age girl knows her parents cannot afford to buy her the expensive formal, but the feelings of sadness, depression, and envy are there just the same. If mother helps her talk these feelings through, the end result can be a closer tie between mother and daughter, instead of an ugly scene where hostile feelings are exchanged.

Find and Correct This Mother's Mistakes

In the following dialogue, the mother will miss four opportunities to use reflective communication. Read carefully and write down each mistake Mom makes and what she should have said. Then compare your answers with the discussion that follows.

John is six and his mother has recently come home from the hospital with a new baby, John's first sibling. As mother is giving the baby a careful sponge bath in the kitchen, John stalks into the room. He glares at them both and then stalks out, kicking a chair as he leaves.

MOM: John, come back in here. What do you mean kicking that chair?

SON: The dumb old chair got in my way.

MOM: Well, just push it out of the way next time. . . . John, is something wrong? You look so upset.

SON: I . . . I . . . I . . . I hate that baby!

MOM: Oh John, no! You don't hate the baby. He's your brother.

SON: I do, too. I wish he'd never never come here!

MOM: Now, John dear, these are terrible things to say. People don't hate their brothers. You should be happy he's here. Why, pretty soon he'll be running around and you'll have a playmate all the time.

SON: I don't want to play with him. I want to play with you and Daddy like we did before. I don't want him. Can't we take him back to the hospital?

MOM: Now John, that's enough of that kind of talk. We aren't taking the baby back anywhere. He's staying here. He's part of the family now and Mommy and Daddy love you both very much.

Mom's Four Mistakes

Sibling rivalry occurs in all families. The only difference is to what degree. In few situations can reflective communication be used more effectively. Yet, in this dialogue the mother consistently misses golden opportunities to help her older child express his thoughts and feelings and to show him she understands. The conversation could have strengthened mother's relationship with John, but instead it left him in painful emotional and intellectual turmoil.

Mother's first mistake was to concern herself foremost with the chair. Obviously, the child was upset; yet, her first response expressed concern for the chair, as though it were more important than John. A more appropriate response to John's kicking the chair and stalking out would have been, "John, you are very angry about something. Please come back in here and tell me what it is."

Mother's second mistake was to deny John's feelings altogether when he said he hates the baby. Feelings should never be denied. When a child confesses that he has a certain feeling, no matter how shocked we are, telling him he doesn't have or shouldn't have that feeling will not make it go away. Feelings are not bad or good. They just are! The actions emerging from feelings can be good or bad, but not the feelings themselves. Mother could have simply said, "You don't like the baby."

Next, mother tried to make John feel guilty for his feelings and for his wish (thought) that the baby had never come. "These are terrible things to say," she tells John. Mother had many other options. She could have reflected, "You wish things could be like they were before," or "You feel very jealous of the baby," or "You're angry at Mommy for bringing the baby home," or simply "You think it would be nice if the baby hadn't come."

In her fourth mistake, mother closed the door on John expressing himself again. "Now John," she says, "that's enough of that kind of talk." Mother could have used reflective communication and said, "You think it was more fun before the baby came," or "It makes you feel lonely to have me spend so much time with the baby," or "It makes you sad that our games aren't quite the same since the baby came." But she didn't. As a result, it will be difficult for John to summon the courage again to tell his mother what he is thinking and feeling. Have no doubt, though, John's thoughts and feelings will find expression. John may break dishes, throw tantrums, become increasingly sullen or try to hurt the baby, but he will express himself somehow.

Were you able to determine where the mother failed to take advantage of opportunities for reflective communication? If not, go back and re-study the lesson. If you did detect and correct the mother's mistakes, then continue on in your manual.

Summary, Warnings, and "Graduation Exercise"

Let's review briefly some of the rules governing reflective communication:
1. Listen carefully to what your child is saying.
2. Condense your child's message to its most vital meaning. (Reflective responses are usually shorter than the child's statement.)
3. Don't simply parrot what the child has said. If possible, use synonyms.
4. Reflect what the child is thinking and feeling, not what you are thinking and feeling.
5. Be selective about when and how you use reflective communication. Keep in mind that it loses some of its effect if used constantly, especially with older children.
6. Statements of understanding (reflective responses) should precede advice, instruction or probing.
7. Relax; reflect in a way comfortable for you.
8. Don't be afraid to try.

Remember, too, the benefits of reflective communication:
1. Helps build a relationship of love and trust
2. Has the power to calm your child
3. Opens channels of communication between parent and child so they can talk rather than fight
4. Enhances the child's self-esteem. (He must be worth something if Mom and Dad take time to listen to him and do not consider his feelings and thoughts improper, stupid or inappropriate.)
5. Helps the child develop a "feeling vocabulary"
6. The child develops more self-control as he learns to express himself in an appropriate manner using a feeling vocabulary.

A Beginning, Not the End

A few reflective responses can begin a conversation, but the conversation does not have to stay strictly at a reflective level. Reflective communication may just get the conversation started.

Keep in mind that reflective communication can be used when your children are happy as well as upset. Respond with enthusiasm to your children's joys and triumphs. For example, when a girl returns all aglow from her first prom and tells her mother all about the exciting evening, her mother may reply, "This has really been a special evening for you, hasn't it, dear? You sound like you're on top of the world." How much more this can mean to their relationship than if the mother were to respond, "I'm glad you had a nice time, sweetheart. See you in the morning."

Graduation Exercise

In this final exercise, respond to each of the following statements using reflective communication. Read the child's statement, verbalize a response, and then turn the page to read several correct responses. Assess whether or not you responded with the appropriate phrasing. Reflective communication responses can vary, but yours should contain certain basic elements: concern, attention to the child's feelings or thoughts, and a desire to show your child that you are interested and want to understand him.

1. Look Mom, I got an A on my test in English.

2. Nobody will be my friend.

3. No matter what I do, I just cannot study for this test.

4. We studied Congress in civics today and I think the system stinks.

5. I am afraid to go to the recital and have everybody watch me.

6. What happens if I make a mistake in front of the whole class?

7. It seems that I always want a lot of praise from people.

8. I hate to cry. I always do.

9. Please don't leave me with the babysitter. I don't like it.

10. But everybody does it.

11. Daddy, the kids hurt my feelings.

12. I don't like you anymore.

13. You treat me as if I were 10 years old, but I'm not.

14. I don't know why I did it; I just did it.

15. You don't care what happens to me, only what your precious neighbors will think.

16. You don't love me and you never have.

Answers to Graduation Exercise

1. That makes you feel proud.
   Hey, you did really well.

2. You feel very lonely.
   You don't have anybody to play with.

3. You're really nervous about this test.
   Sometimes studying can be hard.

4. You are upset about the system.
   You don't think the system works well.

5. It's scary to perform in front of others.

6. You are really anxious about doing well.

7. You feel insecure about yourself.
   You want people to say nice things about you.
   It feels good to get a lot of praise.

8. It's embarrassing to cry in front of others.
   You don't like to cry.

9. You don't want to stay here while Dad and I leave.
   You would rather come with Mom and Dad.

10. If you don't, you really feel left out.

11. That makes you sad.
    The kids have been mean to you.

12. You are really angry at me.
    You feel that I haven't been nice to you.

13. You don't think I understand you.
    You are angry.

14. You did it without knowing why.
    You feel confused about why you did it.

15. You don't think I really care about you.
    You are angry at me.

16. You think I never really cared for you.
    You feel hurt and angry at me.

Post-Test

Under each child's statement write how you would respond using **Reflective Communication.** Some possible responses are on page 33. You will want to compare your post-test responses with those you gave on the pretest when you began this course.

1. I surely had a good time at the ball game.

2. Look, Dad. I cleaned up my room all by myself.

3. Dad, will you stay with me for a little while before I go to sleep?

4. Susy has such beautiful hair. I try and try to make mine look better but it doesn't.

5. You're the best Mom in the whole world.

6. I shouldn't have hit Tommy. It was wrong.

7. But Mom, I don't want my hair in a ponytail. It's my hair anyway.

8. Dad, is this model right? Is it good enough?

9. I want to call Evelyn for a date but . . .

10. My teachers never give me a chance. They seem to get angry at me for no reason at all.

11. I want to button my own coat. I'm big now.

12. Dad, I don't want to make this decision. You make it instead.

13. I don't think I'll ever get over Bill. How could he ever drop me for that Susan Chalmers?

14. Everybody else gets to go to the city. You just don't trust me.

15. I sure am glad that you and Dad love me enough to set rules for me. Jody's parents don't and she wishes they did.

16. Mom, you are always telling me what to do.

17. If I want to stay out late, you can't stop me.

18. You didn't treat Janet like this when she was my age.

19. You never listen to me.

20. What I do is my business, not yours.

Answers to
Post-Test and Pretest

1. The ball game was a lot of fun.
2. You really feel proud.
   You did a good job on your room.
3. You like it when I sit with you for a while.
   It feels good to be together—just the two of us.
4. You'd like to have hair like Susy's.
   It's discouraging to try to do something and fail.
5. You think I'm pretty neat, huh?
   I love you, too.
6. You are sorry you hit Tommy.
   Yep. Hitting is wrong.
7. You would like to wear your hair another way.
   You feel I'm treating you like a baby.
8. You're not sure how well you have done.
9. It's scary to ask a girl out.
   You would like to date Evelyn.
10. You feel picked on.
    You are having problems with your teachers.
11. You want to do it yourself.
12. You would feel better if I made the decision.
    It's scary to make decisions.
13. It hurts to lose your boyfriend.
    Bill left you for Susan Chalmers.
14. You think you should be able to go to the city.
    You feel we don't have faith that you will drive safely.
15. It's nice to feel loved.
    Rules do make life easier.
16. You think I never let you do things on your own.
    You don't feel that I trust you.
17. You're angry at me for setting a curfew.
    You don't think the rules are fair.
    You are really upset about this, aren't you?
18. The way w   t toward you seems unfair.
    Janet had it better than you.
19. You think I just don't hear what you say to me.
    That makes you angry.
    It hurts you to think that I don't listen to you.
20. You think I shouldn't meddle in your affairs.
    You'd like me to stay out of your life.
    You're feeling pressured to do what I want you to do.

A Final Word of Caution

If your relationship with your children has motivated you to see what this workbook has to offer, you may well be the kind of person who has looked into all of the current approaches to child-rearing and sampled their techniques. You may feel you have failed repeatedly to create the family life you want.

Reflective communication, when used properly, works so very often. The catch, however, is that there are many times when, like every other parent—like us, the authors of this manual—you do not want to use the techniques. You are just too angry, too shocked, too frightened, too hurt. When this happens, try not to blame yourself or the technique.

If you have trouble at first, don't give up. Don't assume that the principles are ineffective. Rather, re-study the material in the workbook and get a firmer grip on it.

Remember: To the degree that you use reflective communication, you'll be that much more in touch and in tune with your children. And that's where you have to start if you want to succeed as a parent.

LESSON TWO: CONSEQUENCES

An Alternative to Punishment

Pretest

Please take the following test, circling *T* if you think the statement is true and *F*, if you think it is false. Once you have completed the lesson, you will take the test again. By comparing your two sets of responses, you will see how much you have learned and how your opinions have changed.

1. Children can learn to accept responsibility for their own actions.   T   F

2. To discipline a child effectively a certain amount of punishment must be used.   T   F

3. Even preverbal children can learn that their actions have consequences.   T   F

4. Children must learn that parents are older and wiser, so it's all right to say, "I told you so."   T   F

5. Using candy and toys to coax a child to behave may not be the best way to control him, but it has no long-range negative effects.   T   F

6. Just your tone of voice can change a consequence into a punishment.   T   F

7. The child who is constantly bribed to behave would most likely ask which question(s) before deciding to take an action.
   a. How will this help me get ahead?   T   F
   b. How will this help me grow and develop?   T   F
   c. What's in it for me?   T   F
   d. How will this help someone else?   T   F

8. A child should never be given an allowance.   T   F

9. A consequence is that event which is either the natural, logical or prearranged result of the event preceding it.   T   F

10. A child's good behavior should have its roots in his desire to please, belong, cooperate, and contribute.   T   F

11. Punishment is something the parent does *to* the child which emphasizes the parent's personal power and superiority.   T   F

12. To discipline a child means to teach him to behave acceptably.   T   F

Situation

Larry, age five, and his friends are playing in the backyard. Larry has been teasing the other children, throwing sand and grabbing toys. Mother has asked Larry to stop abusing the other children and to share his toys; however, Larry continues to misbehave.

Response # 1

Mother grabs Larry's arm. "Why can't you behave yourself?" she screams. "You're being plain nasty. Now play nicely or I'll give you a spanking."

(Later, mother does spank Larry who cries for a while and then throws some more sand.)

Response # 2

Mother pleads with Larry, "Why can't you play nicely, dear? It's no fun to fight. Listen, if you'll play nicely, we'll go for ice cream after supper tonight."

Response # 3

Mother calmly approaches Larry. "It seems that you can't play nicely, Larry. You will have to come inside for a while." If Larry balks, Mother adds, "Would you like to walk or would you rather I carry you?" (Larry stays inside for 10 minutes. Then he is given another chance to play outside nicely. If he misbehaves again, he is brought in for a longer period and then for the rest of the day.)

Responses 1, 2, and 3 illustrate various ways to discipline a child. A parent can:

Punish

Reward

or use a technique called

Consequences.

Most parents agree that discipline is a desirable thing. We want to teach our children to abide voluntarily by the rules of our homes and those of society. We know, too, that children desire discipline as a sign of parental love and concern. The question then is not whether children should be disciplined, but rather what is the best way to enforce and maintain discipline.

Traditionally, most parents have relied on a system of punishment and rewards to enforce rules and gain the cooperation of their children; however, the system is often ineffective. A spanking may stop little Johnny from whining and fussing through dinner one night, but the next night the scene is likely to repeat itself. A lollipop may quiet a child temporarily, but rewards, like punishments, don't bring lasting results. Think about the things you spanked or yelled at your child for today. How many times have you bribed, yelled or spanked for the very same reason? *If a child must be spanked or bribed over and over again for the same thing, doesn't that tell you that the spanking and bribing are not working?*

Discipline Without Punishment and Reward

You can discipline your child without hitting or bribing him. You can teach him to behave acceptably without using punishment or reward. There is an alternative—the technique of Consequences. It teaches a child that he is responsible for the results of his own actions. The consequences of the child's own behavior control him.

Using Consequences, a parent can discipline a child (that is, teach him to follow the rules) without bribing, screaming, threatening, slapping and spanking. Wouldn't your home be a more pleasant place without these things?

Let's take a closer look at Punishment, Rewards, and Consequences and see why Consequences is the better disciplinary tool.

Punishment

Punishment is something the parent *does to the child*, which emphasizes the parent's personal power and superiority. If you spank, slap, or yell at your child; if you send him to his room or suspend his privileges, then you are punishing him.

Is punishment of any kind always wrong? Are there any situations that warrant a spanking? Of course. When a young child is in danger (playing with a light socket, running out into the street, etc.), a slap on the hand or a spanking may be necessary to impress on the child the importance of obeying you. The child who is constantly slapped or spanked, however, will probably see no difference between spilling his juice and playing in the street.

Punishment may successfully change a child's behavior. A child who is frightened enough of spanking, yelling, or restrictions may stop doing what annoys his parents. At least for a while.

So what's wrong with punishment?

1. Punishment does not make your relationship with your child more positive. (Remember, we are discussing punishment, not discipline. Children need and want discipline as proof of your love and concern.)

2. Punishment can act like a "dare" to your child, challenging him to show you that there is nothing you can do to him that will make him change his behavior. The more you punish, the more he retaliates. Parent and child become more interested in proving their power than either teaching or learning.

3. Children want your attention. They would prefer to please you, but sometimes they find it easier to keep your attention by upsetting you. This is especially true of younger children.

Why does a child write on the wall with crayon, splash water out of the tub, use language you have forbidden or hit siblings, *knowing* he will be punished? Often it is because he wants your attention. The attention is negative, it's true, but the parent is involved with the child and that's what the child wants. In this type of situation, punishment can actually encourage the annoying behavior rather than stop it.

4. Another problem with punishment is that parents have to administer it and parents are people!

Today, Timmy may spill his juice and be reprimanded lightly by his mother; tomorrow he may spill his juice and be spanked by her. Being human, parents are not always consistent. Punishment is often random and unplanned. It is administered as the mood and moment dictate. So a sassy remark gets a stern warning Monday morning and a slap Monday night.

Rewards— The Other Side of the Coin

By rewards we mean tangible things such as candy, clothes, a new toy, as well as special privileges like staying up or out later. We are not discussing emotional rewards. We are not talking about giving or withholding approval, but giving or withholding chewing gum.

Can any lasting change in behavior be brought about by bribery? Can good habits be established permanently by dangling a new toy in front of a child?

What a Lollipop Can Do for You

1. Gain temporary cooperation.

Obviously special treats can get a child to cooperate with you temporarily. If you're a weary mother who is trying to shop with fussy children, temporary relief may be all you want.

2. Learning can be encouraged with rewards.

Research has shown that while many children learn faster when encouraged with expressions of love and approval, some learn faster when rewarded with something tangible.

3. Rewards can encourage a child to begin a new activity.

Sometimes rewards can motivate a child to start an activity that he later finds pleasurable for itself. The rewards can then be dispensed with. One mother reports that she coaxed her four-year-old into preschool every morning by promising to give him M & M's when he came home. The child was frightened of the new situation and balked at going to class; however, his love for candy-coated chocolate prevailed. Soon he felt comfortable in class and was enjoying preschool. Mom discontinued the M & M's.

What a Lollipop Can Do To Your Child

Bringing up baby on bribes can have a profound effect on your child's whole attitude toward life. He will learn to gauge his actions and achievements, not by the sense of accomplishment they give him, the approval they bring, or the happiness they give to others, but by what he *gets*. "What's in it for me?" will be his philosophy. He becomes monstrously materialistic.

MOM: Will you help me cut out this pattern, Sue?
SUE: May I stay out later on Friday?.

DAD: Let's get that new fencing up today, son.
SON: How much an hour are you going to pay me?

The "What's in it for me" child gains satisfaction from getting, not giving.

Parents who use rewards to gain cooperation may find themselves locked into a pattern of ever-increasing demands from their children. Five-year-old Sally starts in on her mother as soon as they enter a store:

SALLY: May I have a treat if I'm very good and don't touch anything on the shelves?"

MOM: "We'll see, dear."

SALLY: "I want gum."

MOM: "Let's wait and see how you behave."

SALLY: "Can't I have a balloon?"

MOM: "We'll see."

SALLY: "I want this," Sally says, picking something from a shelf.

MOM: (reprimanding) "You said you wouldn't touch anything."

SALLY: "I won't do it again. May I still have a treat?"

And so Sally whines and coaxes the entire time and *every time* she and Mom go shopping.

A child's good behavior should have its roots in his desire to please, belong, cooperate, and contribute. The child who is constantly bribed does not value approval, achievement or self-esteem as much as he values candy, toys or a new car. His is a value system that can easily lead to a maladjusted, unhappy, and unfulfilled adulthood.

A Word About Allowances

Money is an important aspect of our everyday lives. Children must learn how to handle it properly and many parents believe than an allowance is a good way to teach money management. It can be if the allowance is given and received with the right attitude.

An allowance should not be payment for chores. We pay hired help. A family member shares the benefits of a clean, well-kept home. Are we just playing with words here? No! There *is* a difference between telling a child that he won't get his allowance if he doesn't take out the garbage and explaining to him that those in the family who do not contribute, will not receive. This difference is vital. If it is not recognized, allowances can become bribes and add to the "What's in it for me" syndrome.

Consequences

A consequence is that event which is either the natural, logical or prearranged result of the event preceding it.

Would you like to read that again?

A consequence is that event which is either the natural, logical or prearranged result of the event preceding it.

That may sound complicated, but you probably understand consequences already. You just may not have thought of them as a way of disciplining children.

Exercise:

See if you can match the following examples to the different kinds of consequences (natural, logical, and prearranged). There are several examples of each kind of consequence.

Place letters here

Natural Consequences _____

Logical Consequences _____

Prearranged Consequences _____

a. If Betsy touches a hot stove, she will be burned.

b. A bike continually left out overnight is likely to get stolen.

c. Mary and her parents have agreed that any belongings left out of place after 9:00 p.m. will be collected and put in a box, not to be removed until the following Monday.

d. If Johnny is still undressed by the time Mom is ready to go out, he will not be able to go with her.

e. A lunchbox left dirty overnight will be smelly and repulsive by morning.

f. If Mom has to clean up Jenny's room in the morning, she will not have time that evening to hem Jenny's new dress for the next day.

g. Children are likely to stub their toes if they play barefoot.

h. Damp clothes left in a heap long enough will mildew.

i. Bobby and his parents agreed that if he failed to clean his hamster's cage once a week, the pet would have to go.

j. A child who refuses to eat dinner and receives no evening snacks will be hungry by breakfast.

Now check your answers against the following key.

Natural Consequences	a e h j
Logical Consequences	b d f g
Prearranged Consequences	c i

How did you do? Were you surprised by how much you know about consequences already? Now we'll define each type of consequence. At the same time, we'll discuss the answers to the exercise you just completed.

Natural Consequence: An inevitable result that occurs naturally, without assistance.

a. Touch something hot and you *will* be burned.
e. Leave particles of tuna fish sandwich in a lunchbox overnight and it *will* be smelly by morning.
h. Damp clothing left in a pile long enough *will* mildew.
j. If you don't eat, you *will* get hungry.

Logical Consequence: A result that has a rational connection to the event preceding it; the result makes sense in the context of what is considered normal or acceptable behavior.

b. A bike left out overnight, night after night, may never be stolen, but it is rational to assume that it is likely to be stolen. Getting stolen is a logical—if not inevitable—consequence of the bike being left out.
d. In our society it is not considered acceptable to take a naked child (or one dressed only in underpants) to the store. Therefore, if four-year-old Johnny does not get dressed, it is logical that he cannot go with Mom to the store.
f. There are only so many hours in a day and Mom has a certain number of chores to do within that time. Every member of the family has a claim on some of Mom's time—including Mom! It is logical to say, then, that if Mom must spend time cleaning Jenny's room, she very well may not have time to hem Jenny's dress. (Logical consequences often assume that family members need each other's help, that they are interrelated. If one member will not do his part, then the others must fill in for him. As a result, they may not have time, energy or resources to assist the non-contributor later.)
g. Chances are that a child will stub his toe if he doesn't wear shoes.

Prearranged Consequence: A result decided on by both parent and child. It may or may not be natural or logical, but it has been *discussed* and *agreed* upon by both.

c. Mary's math book is on the living room table when Mom walks by at 9:15 p.m. Into the box it goes. Mary's book does not naturally or even logically find itself impounded until Monday; however, this consequence was agreed upon by Mary and her parents. It is prearranged and understood by all family members.
i. When Bobby asks for a pet hamster, his parents agree to get him one on the condition that he clean the cage once a week. Bobby knows and understands what the consequence of not caring for the hamster will be. The consequence is prearranged.

Don't get hung up on terms.

We have discussed three different types of consequences to help you see the variety of alternatives there are to punishment and reward. This division of consequences into natural, logical, and prearranged is not absolute. The three types often blend around the edges. Don't get hung up on terms. Don't be stymied trying to decide what type of consequence to use, terrified you may make a mistake.

BETTER PARENTS, BETTER CHILDREN

Relax; let your imagination flow. Ask yourself, "What will happen if I don't interfere?" and the natural or logical consequence of an action will become apparent. Toys broken through misuse will not be replaced and the child will be minus a plaything. Clothes not put into the hamper won't get washed. Children who throw toys will hurt each other. This last consequence is not acceptable so you must interfere. Either the offending child or the toys must be removed from the situation.

A child who insists on playing in the street may be hit by a car. This is also an unacceptable consequence, so the child must play inside. Sometimes, problems don't generate useable consequences on their own. Then, the parents and child may agree upon a prearranged consequence.

If you agree that slapping a child or handing him a piece of candy is not the best way to discipline him, you may still wonder, why choose Consequences as the alternative disciplinary tool?

Consequences is not the only positive form of discipline available. It cannot be used in all situations. Still there are many reasons to recommend the technique:

1. The proper use of Consequences can motivate a child to change his behavior.
   Nobody wants to be hungry, left behind or have his possessions impounded until Monday. Children bring such calamities on themselves when they:
   (a) engage their parents in a power struggle
                  or
   (b) misbehave to get attention

But a child cannot show his power over or get attention from a consequence. When consequences are used, misbehaving becomes less profitable for your child: proper behavior, more profitable.

2. Consequences teach responsibility.
   By allowing consequences to discipline your child, you teach him an important lesson in life: He is responsible for his own actions. He doesn't do something just to please you; nor does he avoid doing something because he is afraid of punishment. He chooses to behave in a certain way and then accepts the consequences, good or bad.

3. Consequences build a better relationship between parent and child.
   The *more* you use consequences, the *less* you use punishment. As a result, your children don't see you as someone who constantly hurts, shames or restricts them.
   The *more* you use consequences, the *less* you use bribes. As a result, your children don't look upon you as a patsy to be coaxed and conned into forking over goodies.

4. Discipline with consequences helps everyone stay calmer.
   Flaring tempers, angry words, misunderstandings, and hurt feelings are far less likely when consequences are used.

5. Consequences put the accent on learning.
   Children learn that fire will burn them and ice will chill them; that if they misbehave, they will be removed from the group.

A
Problem
with
Consequences

As you continue with this lesson, try to be sensitive to the realization that your attitude can keep you from giving consequences a chance to work. A punishing attitude through which you communicate disgust or anger by the tone of your voice can change consequences into punishment. Can you see the difference in attitude in these two examples?

Example #1

DAD: Tom, the grass needs mowing. Would you please take care of it before you go out this afternoon?

TOM: Sure, Dad.
       (Two hours later the grass is still not mowed.)

DAD: Where are you going, son?

TOM: To play ball with the guys.

DAD: I'm sorry Tom, but the grass isn't mowed yet.

TOM: I'll do it later, okay.

DAD: No, Tom; it will have to be done before you go.

TOM: Oh come on, Dad; the game is starting.

DAD: Like everyone else, Tom, you must do your Saturday job before you go out.

TOM: Oh Dad, come on; I'll do it later. There won't be enough guys to have a game. Come on, I'll miss the game if I mow it now.

DAD: Not if you hurry. (Dad is pleasant, but firm. He goes to another room and removes himself from the conflict.)

Example #2

DAD: Tom, the grass needs mowing. Would you please take care of it before you go out?

TOM: Sure.

(Later)

DAD: Where are you going?

TOM: To play ball with the guys.

DAD: Oh no, you're not. You haven't mowed the grass yet.

TOM: I'll do it later, okay.

DAD: The heck you will. You've had all morning to mow that lawn and you're not going any place until it is done.

TOM: Oh come on, Dad; the game is starting!

DAD: Tough luck. Now get to it. You know mowing the lawn is your Saturday job. The rule is nobody goes off until his job is done.

TOM: I'll do it when I get back.

DAD: Oh, sure. I've heard that before. Now quit stalling; stop being so lazy and get to it.

TOM: Oh crud!

DAD: I'm telling you to get to that lawn!

BETTER PARENTS, BETTER CHILDREN

Analysis

Can you complete the analysis of these two examples? Choose words from the list provided and fill in the blanks. All the words should be used, but only once.

In Example #1, Dad acts as an
_____ of the rules. He is not
_____ Tom. No one is being
_____ to Tom. Tom
_____ the family rule about
Saturday jobs and he has_____
not to do his job. The _____
is that he will not play ball Saturday
afternoon until he mows the lawn.

mean

understands

chosen

consequence

punishing

enforcer

In Example #2, Dad _____
Tom. He raises his voice. He calls Tom
_____. Dad_____ Tom in
a _____ struggle. In Example Two
it is not Tom vs. the _____. It is Tom
vs. _____. The interaction
creates _____
and _____.

rules

power

engages

Dad

resentment

berates

lazy

anger

The paragraphs should read:

In Example #1, Dad acts as an *enforcer* of the rules. He is not *punishing* Tom. No one is being *mean* to Tom. Tom *understands* the family rule about Saturday jobs and he has *chosen* not to do his job. The *consequence* is that he will not play ball Saturday afternoon until he mows the lawn.

In Example #2, Dad *berates* Tom. He raises his voice. He calls Tom *lazy*. Dad *engages* Tom in a *power* struggle. In Example Two, it is not Tom vs. the *rules*. It is Tom vs. *Dad*. The interaction creates *anger* and *resentment*.

Just as a punishing attitude can turn consequences into punishment, a tendency to entice can turn consequences into bribery.

Study the following two examples. Can you see the difference?

Example #1

(Terry is a 13-year-old girl.)

MOM: Terry, please clean up your room.
TERRY: I don't want to.
MOM: Please, Terry, I don't want to have to get nasty about this.
TERRY: I can't; it's too messed up. I don't know where to start.
MOM: Look, Terry. If you'll clean up your room and keep it neat, we'll see about that slumber party you've been wanting to have.
TERRY: Well, okay.

Example #2

MOM: Terry, would you please clean up your room?

TERRY: I can't; it's too messed up. I don't know where to start.

MOM: It's your room, dear.

(Later)

TERRY: Mom, I can't find my Keds or my tennis racquet.

MOM: They're in your room somewhere, Terry.

(Later, Terry is doing her homework at the dining room table.)

MOM: Terry, you'll have to take your papers and books back to your room.

TERRY: There's no place to spread them out in there. I can't work at my desk.

MOM: Your room is yours to keep as you please, dear, but the dining room is the family's and you have no right to mess it up. Now, please take your books to your room.

(Later)

TERRY: Mom, make Billy and his dumb little friend go outside to play. We want to talk in here.

BILLY: We were watching Batman first.

MOM: Can't you girls talk over the TV set?

TERRY: No.

MOM: Then I suggest you go to Terry's room to talk.

TERRY: (aside to Mom) I can't take them in there.

MOM: That could be embarrassing.

Analysis

Can you complete the analysis of these two examples? Choose words from the list provided and fill in the blanks. All the words should be used, but only once.

In Example #1, Mother is_____.

Terry a_____. Some parents con

themselves into thinking that "_____

you'll clean up your room,_____ I'll

let you have a party" is a _____

consequence. But it's not. It is a bribe

and contributes to the "_____ _____

_____ _____ _____" philosophy.

what's

if

for

it

then

bribe

offering

prearranged

in

me

47

In Example #2, Mother allows a
_____ consequence to occur. When
a room is not _____ on a regular
basis, it becomes_____ to live
in. The room is_____. Mom
literally closes the door on it. She
does not_____and she does not
go in.

Eventually Terry will realize
that Mom is truly_____.
She is ____going to clean up Terry's
room. She is not going to_____
Terry to clean up her room. Terry is
the only one_____. Nobody
else has even mentioned the room for
weeks! It becomes_____to
Terry that the room is her_____
and_____must keep it neat or
_____ the _____.
_____the room has
been cleaned, Mom can comment on how
nice it looks. But she_____
saying, "It's about_____!"

Terry may also get her_____,
but the party and the room are not
_____together. The general
feeling in the home should be: You
_____and you_____,
rather than you will be_____with
a party for cleaning your room.

discussed
unconcerned
responsibility
cleaned
suffering
Terry's
contribute
natural
after
paid
comment
clear
unpleasant
not
party
suffer
time
bribe
avoids
receive
consequences
she

The paragraphs should read:

In Example #1, Mother is *offering* Terry a *bribe*. Some parents con themselves into thinking that "*If* you'll clean up your room, *then* I'll let you have a party" is a *prearranged* consequence. But it's not. It is a bribe and contributes to the "*What's in it for me*" philosophy.

In Example #2, Mother allows a *natural* consequence to occur. When a room is not *cleaned* on a regular basis it becomes *unpleasant* to live in. The room is *Terry's*. Mom literally closes the door on it. She does not *comment* and she does not go in.

Eventually Terry will realize that Mom is truly *unconcerned*. She is *not* going to clean up Terry's room. She is not going *to bribe* Terry to clean up her room. Terry is the only one *suffering*. Nobody else has even mentioned the room for weeks! It becomes *clear* to Terry that the room is her *responsibility* and *she* must keep it neat or *suffer* the *consequences*.

After the room has been cleaned, Mom can comment on how nice it looks. But, she *avoids* saying, "It's about *time*!" Terry may also get her *party*, but the party and the room are not *discussed* together. The general feeling in the home should be: You *contribute* and you *receive*, rather than you will be *paid* with a party for cleaning your room.

A
Thin
Line

As we said before, the line between consequences and punishment/reward is a thin one. Here are four rules to help you avoid crossing over the line.

1. *Adjust your attitude.* Your true feelings communicate themselves. If you want to punish your child (not discipline, but punish), then your tone of voice and choice of words will deliver the message loud and clear. At the end of the "Terry and her room" example, Mom says, "That could be embarrassing." Think of all the ways that sentence could be said. *Only* if it is said without sarcasm is the parent using consequences.

2. *Avoid phrases like these:*
   "I told you this would happen!"
   "Why can't you do what I tell you?"
   "Why didn't you listen to me?"
   "Well, you asked for it!"

Phrases like these turn consequences into punishment. The idea is to let the child learn from experiencing the consequences of his actions. If you provoke him, berate him or nag him, his attention switches from the consequence to you! He is no longer learning because his energy is directed toward being angry or hurt or toward retaliating.

3. *Don't give rewards on an if-then basis.* It is one thing to say, "When you've finished your work, let's go for a root beer." It's another to say, "**If** you'll do your work, then I'll buy you a root beer."

4. *Use what you've learned in Lesson I.* Reflective communication will often prove useful when you are responding to a child who is suffering the consequences of his actions. For example, imagine that your son has lost his bike through his own carelessness:

SON: But I can't play with the guys if I don't have a bike. They can't wait for me all the time.

PARENT: It's hard to keep up with the other boys without a bike.

Reflective communication allows you to respond without punishing or rewarding your child. You aren't making punishing remarks like those we suggested you avoid in Rule 2. At the same time, you aren't sympathizing with the child to such an extent that you reward him for his carelessness. Even though you aren't going to replace the bike, you can still empathize with the child's sadness. After all, the boy is learning a hard lesson!

Three
Exercises

Keeping the rules just listed in mind, complete the following three exercises.

Exercise I

Try to distinguish between consequences, punishment, and reward by writing C, P or R in the space following each statement. The correct answers are on **page** 51.

1. Honestly, Andrew! I told you that pan was still hot. Look at that burn! Why can't you listen? _____

2. Since you can't play with the other children nicely, Ralph, you'll have to come inside.
3. If you pick up your toys, Linda, then I'll take you to the park. _____

4. Oh, Andrew, what a nasty burn! I'll bet that hurts. _____

5. I've told you a hundred times not to hit other children! Now, get into this house! _____
6. I warned you that you'd break the doll house by sitting on it, Ann. And don't think I'm going to buy you a new one. _____

7. If you pull three A's this semester, son, I'll get you a car of your own. _____

8. One more smart remark, Miss, and I'll slap your mouth. (Child talks back again; parent slaps child's mouth.) _____

9. I'm sorry your doll house is broken, Ann. _____

10. Patty, I do not have to carry on a conversation with someone who cannot speak nicely. _____

Answers to
Exercise I

1. P
2. C
3. R
4. C
5. P
6. P
7. R
8. P
9. C
10. C

How did you do? If you had trouble distinguishing between consequences, punishment, and reward, read through the lesson again. If you got at least seven correct, then continue on to the next exercise.

Exercise II

Study the following examples. In some, the parents have used consequences well. In others, they have made mistakes. In the space provided, write either correct, if you feel the parent has made good use of consequences, or incorrect, if you discern a mistake. If you write incorrect, then underline the sentence or sentences in the example that you think contain an error. When you finish, compare your answers with those on page 54.

Example # 1

Susan is a fussy eater. Tonight, as usual, she is playing with her food. The rest of the family is about finished eating. Susan's family has had a conference. Together they agreed that everyone must eat what is on his dinner plate in order to receive dessert or a snack of any kind later in the evening.

DADDY: (with great patience) Susan, please eat your dinner. If you don't, you'll be hungry. Do you want to be hungry? Remember, if you don't eat, then no dessert or snacks.

SUSAN: I'm not hungry, Daddy.

DADDY: Okay, but remember: no dessert or snacks.

Answer: _____

Example # 2

Toby is five years old. Sick as an infant and toddler, Toby developed an atittude of helplessness. Now well and able to do things for himself, Toby keeps his family in servitude by continuing to appear helpless. One morning Mom lays out Toby's clothes.

MOM: Get dressed dear and then you can go out and play.

TOBY: I can't; you have to help me.

MOM: (pleasantly) I have my own work to do, Toby.

Mom then leaves the room. If Toby attempts to go outside undressed, mother brings him back inside and explains that it it not acceptable for children to play outside undressed. Mom goes about her own business, refusing to be drawn into an argument. She remains firm about the need for Toby to get dressed before he goes outside to play.

Answer: _____

Example # 3

Jerry is a forgetful 10-year-old. Several times a week Mom must take his lunch to school for him. Mom has pleaded, scolded, and punished, but Jerry still forgets his lunch. One morning Mom decides to use consequences. "Here is your lunch, Jerry," she says calmly. "It is your lunch, not mine. It is your responsibility to take your lunch to school with you each day. If you forget it, I will not bring it to you."

The next day Jerry forgets his lunch again. Mom does *not* take it to school. Without lunch, Jerry gets hungry. (Mom may find it necessary to seek the school's assistance so that Jerry is not given lunch or lunch money.) Jerry is angry when he gets home. "Why didn't you bring me my lunch?" Jerry demands.

"I'm sorry you were hungry, Jerry," Mother replies calmly. "I hope you've learned something from this."

Answer: _____

Example # 4

Thirteen-year-old Marcy stands on a stool while her mother tries to mark a hem on the dress she is wearing. As usual, Marcy is not being very cooperative. Fitting sessions with Marcy are a hassle for Mom. Today she decides to try consequences.

MOM: Marcy, please stand still. I can't mark this properly if you don't.

MARCY: (shifting her weight) It's hard to stand up straight for so long.

MOM: I know. But if you don't stand straight the marks will all be crooked.

MARCY: (shifting again) Would you please hurry up, Mom. This is such a drag.

MOM: (closing her pin book and gathering up her equipment) You can get down now.

MARCY: But you haven't finished marking the hem yet.

MOM: I have spent all the time I can for today on sewing, dear.

MARCY: But I was going to wear this dress tomorrow.

MOM: You'll have to find something else.

Answer: _____

Answers to
Exercise II

Example # 1 is *incorrect*. Everything Daddy said should be underlined. He threatens Susan with hunger. He attempts to bribe her with dessert. The family position on mealtime has been thoroughly discussed at a family council. *Nothing* need be said at meals. Children will gladly suffer hunger if it gets them attention all through dinner and if they know you are suffering with them. You must be genuinely unconcerned! Eating is the child's responsibility. You cannot eat for him.

Example · # 2 is *correct*. Mom remains pleasant, but firm. She does not argue with Toby. It is painful for parents to watch their children struggle, but excessive assistance and pity for the "helpless" child will not help him at all in the long run.

Example # 3 is *incorrect*. You should have underlined the following two sentences: *"If you forget it, I will not bring it to you,"* and *"I hope you've learned something from this."* Read through the example omitting these two sentences and Mom makes excellent use of consequences. If she sticks to her guns, Jerry will stop forgetting his lunch. It's no fun to be hungry, especially if you're not proving anything to anybody. Put the sentences in and Mom hurls the gauntlet at Jerry. She challenges him to a duel. She is not unconcerned about his lunch at all. She is using Consequences as a power tool. Jerry will show her. He can forget his lunch if he wants to. Mom will show him. She'll just let him starve.

Example # 4 is *correct*. Marcy is 13 years old. She does not need to be told by Mom that she is the reason the marking took so much time. Don't underestimate her. Marcy knows she caused the delay and now she will suffer the consequences. Mom does not need to plead, lecture or scold anymore. All she has to do is withdraw. She has other things to do.

Mom could explain to Marcy that she will not work in an atmosphere of unpleasantness. But, she does not need to cite Marcy as the cause of the unpleasantness or threaten that she will not finish the dress. Marcy knows who causes the unpleasantness. She can figure out that if Mom doesn't work on the dress either she will never get to wear it or have to finish it herself. Both are consequences that Mom can safely allow to occur.

How did you do? If you were unable to recognize the mistakes, re-study the rules on page 49. Then go on to Exercise III.

Exercise III

You have now completed several exercises aimed at teaching you to use consequences. Do you think you can do it? Let's see.

You will be presented with a situation and a child's remark. In the space provided, write what you would *say* or *do* in response.

Don't get flustered and go blank. Relax. There are many correct responses. Have you noticed how often reflective communication works well? Sometimes removing the child from a situation he can't handle acceptably is the answer. Sometimes you should withdraw. At times, no response is the right response. And remember how we talked about letting your imagination flow? Try to picture the natural or logical result of your child's action. Is it a consequence you can allow your child to suffer without serious injury occurring? Will your child learn a useful lesson if you allow the consequence to occur? If so, then the consequence is acceptable. Let it happen.

When you have checked your answers with the answer key and made corrections, read through the dialogues with someone else. Reciting the right responses out loud is excellent preparation for using consequences with your child.

Situation # 1

Your two-year-old Megan whines and fusses constantly. She cries at the drop of a hat. She wants her own way and if she doesn't get it she throws a fit. You have tried spanking and scolding; you have been extra patient and loving. You have even tried Reflective Communication. Now you have decided to try Consequences.

PARENT: Want a popsicle, Megan?
MEGAN: I want a red one.
PARENT: There are only purple ones left.
MEGAN: I don't like purple. I want red! Whine, whine, fuss, fuss.
PARENT: _____
MEGAN: Whine, fuss.
PARENT: _____

Situation # 2

You have given four-year-old Ryan all of your odd spoons to use in his sandbox. You caution him that the spoons could be lost easily in the grass if he takes them out of the sandbox. The next day Ryan comes in asking for more spoons.

RYAN: I can't find any of my spoons. May I have some more please?
PARENT: _____
RYAN: But I want more spoons. They're really fun. They make neat shovels. I can dig deep holes. Come on!
PARENT: _____

Situation # 3

Eight-year-old Mike is cleaning fish with a sharp knife. He has your permission to use the knife, but isn't very experienced at cleaning fish. Mike slips and cuts himself.

MIKE: (crying) Ouch! Help, I cut myself.
PARENT: _____

Situation # 4

Eight-year-old Bonnie likes to cook. This is great, but there are several appliances you have asked her not to use without help. The deep fat fryer is one. French fries are planned for tonight and the grease is heating. Bonnie is slicing potatoes and you leave the kitchen for a minute. You hear a shriek and come running back. Bonnie tried dropping potatoes into the fryer and burned herself.

BONNIE: Ouch. Ouch. Ouch. Oh, my hand!

PARENT: _____

_____

(Later, after the burn is cared for)

PARENT: _____

Situation # 5

Your 16-year-old, Ben, has gotten a ticket for speeding:

BEN: It just didn't seem that I was going that fast.

PARENT: _____

Situation # 6

Deb is your family's fussy eater. (Age, if it's over two, doesn't matter here.)

Deb is pushing the food around on her plate. She has been doing that since the meal was served.

PARENT: _____

_____

Deb continues to play with her food.

PARENT: _____

DEB: (the food still on her plate) I'm done. May I be excused?

PARENT: _____   _____

Exercise III: Answers and Discussion

Situation # 1

PARENT: Want a popsicle Megan?

MEGAN: I want a red one.

PARENT: There are only purple ones left.

MEGAN: I don't like purple. I want a red one. Whine, whine, fuss, fuss.

PARENT: Megan, nobody wants to listen to you fuss and cry. From now on, when you fuss and cry and you are not hurt, you will have to go to your room and stay there until you stop.

MEGAN: Fuss, whine.

Parent escorts or carries Megan to her room. (Try extending one of your fingers toward the child and letting her take hold voluntarily. Often small children will follow you willingly if you don't grab their hands.)

PARENT: When you can stop fussing, we'd love to have you come out and be with the rest of the family.

A whining, fussing child is not pleasant to be around. There is a logical connection between acting obnoxious and being asked to leave. If the child will not stay in her room, then remove yourself. Go to your room, lock the door, and read a book. Most children, however, will stay in their rooms if told to firmly and if they know they can come out as soon as they accomplish a set task, like stopping their crying.

Situation # 2

RYAN: I can't find any of my spoons. May I have some more please?

PARENT: I'm sorry, Ryan, but I don't have any more old spoons. I gave you all of them yesterday.

RYAN: But I want more spoons. They're really fun. They make neat shovels. I can dig deep holes. Come on!

PARENT: The spoons were fun, huh? You must be sad they are gone. I'm sorry you don't have them anymore.

Of course, there are many ways you could have responded correctly. The important thing is that you didn't say, "I told you they'd get lost," or "Why can't you keep track of your toys?" Ryan knows what you told him. Don't take the emphasis off the consequences by attacking Ryan. He is now learning a lesson: Toys lost through carelessness are not replaced. A few more experiences like this and he will keep much closer track of his things.

BETTER PARENTS, BETTER CHILDREN

Situation # 3

MIKE: (crying) Ouch! Help, I cut myself.
PARENT: Oh, what a bad cut. Oh, gee, I'll bet that hurts. Sharp knives can really cut you.
          Sharp knives can be so dangerous.

There are so many things you can say here. Exactly what you say depends on your child and how he reacts to being hurt. The important thing is that you make him feel you care that he's been hurt and that you don't say, "Mike, how can you be so stupid?" or "Oh Mike, why can't you be more careful?" Focus on the consequence, not on berating Mike. Make a factual statement about knives. Mike will learn a lesson because he is thinking about what happened, not about how angry he is at you for jumping on him.

Situation # 4

BONNIE: Ouch. Ouch. Ouch. Oh, my hand!
PARENT: Oh, what a nasty burn. That grease gets so hot. It can burn so badly.
          (After the burn is taken care of)
PARENT: Bonnie, you were asked not to use the fryer alone. Since you did not follow our rule, I'm afraid you won't be able to cook in the kitchen for a while. (In a week you give Bonnie another chance. Children need to know they can always try again. If the rule is broken again, however, Bonnie is restricted for a longer period.)

In Situation # 4, you can deal with the consequence of touching hot grease and/or the consequence of disobeying a rule. There are many things you could say about both. The important thing is that you don't rush in and yell, "I told you not to use that fryer alone, you dummy" or "Well, it serves you right. Look at that hand! Why can't you do what you're told?" Rather, you should comment on the consequences of touching hot grease. Then you can leave the lesson there and see if the child has learned enough so that she will obey the rules in the future or you can go on to discuss the consequences of breaking rules.

A child can learn much from this incident: Grease is hot. Mom and Dad don't make idle rules; they make them for a reason. If you can't follow the rules for safety in the kitchen, you can't cook.

If you attack Bonnie, all of her defense mechanisms swing into action. It is hard for a child to be open to learning when she feels defensive, angry, and hurt.

Situation # 5

BEN: It just didn't seem that I was going that fast.
PARENT: Speed can be deceptive. That's why it's important to keep an eye on the speedometer. You didn't do that, so I'm afraid you won't be allowed to drive the car for two weeks. Then we'll talk about you and the car.

There is a logical connection between using something improperly and losing the right to use it at all. By restricting Ben's use of the car, you enforce a logical consequence of his speeding. You might also have had Ben pay for his own ticket. Again, there is an obvious logical connection between receiving a ticket and having to pay the fine.

Ben will certainly survive if you let him suffer these consequences of his action. In addition, paying the fine will help to teach Ben a lesson about speeding. After two weeks, you and Ben can decide on some prearranged consequences, should he misuse the car in the future.

Situation # 6

Deb is pushing the food around on her plate. She has been doing that since the meal was served.

PARENT: (making conversation that has nothing to do with eating). How was school today? What a lovely day it was today!

(Deb continues to play with her food.)

PARENT: Let's go on a picnic this Saturday.

DEB: (the food still on her plate) I'm done. May I be excused?

PARENT: Yes.

It doesn't matter what you say as long as you don't talk about Deb's eating. Talk to Deb about anything else. Talk to her brothers and sisters. Talk to each other. Enjoy your dinner and your dinner hour. Eating her dinner is *her* problem. The tough part for you is to remain calm and stick to your rule about no dessert or snacks if the child doesn't eat her main dish.

How did you do? If you had trouble, re-study the answers to Exercise III. Practice the dialogues out loud.

Five Questions Many People Ask About Consequences

By now you probably have a good idea of what consequences are and how to use them. But before we conclude Lesson II, let's deal with five questions many people have about consequences.

QUESTION: If I must use some kind of physical action to enforce a consequence, does that make it punishment?

ANSWER: Not necessarily. To take a child gently but firmly to his room and put him on his bed or in a chair is enforcing a consequence. To jerk a child to his room and throw or push him inside is punishment.

QUESTION: Can spanking be a prearranged consequence?

ANSWER: Yes. A poor one, but if both parent and child have discussed a situation and agreed that a certain action will result in a spanking, then it is a prearranged consequence.

BETTER PARENTS, BETTER CHILDREN

QUESTION: Can consequences be used to discipline preverbal children?
ANSWER: Yes. Consequences are most effective with young children and even preverbal children. Actions, as well as words, can communicate the idea that certain behaviors have related consequences. Here is an excellent example provided by Lee Salk, Ph.D., reprinted from the Gerber publication, *Growing up with Gerber* 1975.[1]

"Thus . . . it is quite possible to teach an eight- or nine-month-old that it is all right to tear newspapers but not magazines. If you are surprised that a child less than a year old can be disciplined not to tear magazines, while she is allowed to destroy newspapers, let me explain how it's done. Allow your child to approach a coffee table piled with magazines and newspapers. She will begin to play with them and will look at you as she explores the piles to discover your reaction. As she begins to tear a magazine, take it away, say "No" very firmly, and be emphatic in expressing your annoyance so that your displeasure is clearly understood. Simply murmuring, "No" while smiling probably will not register.

"Although you must make your dissatisfaction absolutely clear, do not act so displeased that your child *stops understanding your displeasure and starts becoming afraid*. Now give the magazine back to your child. More than likely, if she has not been frightened into stopping her efforts to learn, she will make another attempt to tear the magazine, and you should react in exactly the same way. Then your child will begin to see the consistent pattern in your behavior. She will probably go on to repeat her action several times in varying ways to establish clearly that you are indeed reacting to what she is doing and that you really mean what you say. Actually she thinks all this is sort of a game!

"To make your point absolutely clear, somewhere along the line you can pick up a newspaper, tear it and then show your child that she may tear the newspaper. After your child has torn the newspaper, she may again try to tear the magazine. You will have to express your displeasure yet again if the magazine is about to be torn. Your child may have to repeat the experiment involving the newspaper and the magazine a number of times before she learns exactly what the rules and regulations that govern this particular behavior are. If you are going to teach her, that is discipline her, not to tear magazines, you will have to allow a lot of time and be very patient if she is to learn and understand."

And so we see that even a baby can understand that tearing magazines has one consequence, while tearing newspapers has another. Even a baby can learn to adjust her behavior to avoid unpleasant consequences.

QUESTION: I get so angry! How can I control myself so I can use consequences?
ANSWER: There is no *one* way to gain control. But, here are three suggestions:
1. Think to yourself, "I can stay in control for one more minute. Anyone can stay in control for one minute, just one more minute." If you repeat this enough times, you'll have several minutes to calm down.
2. Truthfully consider how you would feel if your spouse or a friend yelled at you, struck you or called you names. Many adults, whose feelings are easily hurt, think nothing of attacking a child in a way that would destroy them. They just don't really consider children people.

[1]Copyright material is courtesy of Gerber Products Company, *Growing up with Gerber* 1975.

60

3. Understand that to many children getting a spanking is one way of winning the game. If they can't get what they want right now, the next best thing is to egg Mom or Dad on into hitting them. Big adult has to hit small child to get compliance. You lose, big adult! Children have expressed the idea to me regularly. Think about it. Realizing who is really the victor could keep you from blowing your top and hitting your child next time.

QUESTION: Is there a set pattern, a series of steps that I can follow in using consequences in my home?

ANSWER: No, the technique of Consequences requires flexibility. No **one** series of steps could possibly fit all situations; however, here is a list of things to consider when using consequences:

1. *Use your imagination.* Ask yourself, "What would happen if the child continues a behavior or takes an action?"
2. *If a misbehavior reoccurs frequently, then discuss it with the child.* Explain to him what the consequences of his actions will be. Don't threaten, just inform.
3. *Let acceptable consequences happen.* Let the child lose that favorite toy. Let him go to school without his lunch and be hungry. It's hard, but it's best in the long run.
4. *If you must act as an enforcer, do so firmly, but without anger.*
5. *After the child has paid the consequences, give him another chance.* People must feel they can try again.
6. *Don't feel guilty.* If a consequence was prearranged, then the child knew what he was in for when he decided to do what he did. If he doesn't like the consequences, he won't choose to do it again. Of course, you may feel sad that your child must suffer a hungry night, a day without playmates, or a missed outing. But remember, he may gain a lifetime of responsible behavior.

After completing this lesson, some of you still probably won't use consequences to discipline your children. Why? You may resist because:

Punishment and rewards are quicker and easier. They take less time, thought, and effort. They may not work in the long run, but they get temporary compliance. You accomplish something fast.

When you're right, you want your child to know it! You want your child to acknowledge that you knew what you were talking about. It's so hard not to say, "I told you so!"

Consequences don't work in every conceivable situation. Of course! Nothing does! But some people won't try anything unless it's guaranteed to be successful, no matter what.

You want to exercise your power. Consciously or unconsciously you desire to control the people and events around you. You don't really care whether your child gains knowledge or learns to accept responsibility. He's your child and you'll show him you can make him do what you want!

You hate the idea that your child might "get away" with something. Actually, when you use consequences, your child is **not** getting away with anything. It's true you're not punishing him. But you are disciplining him.

A Final Word

Parents want to see their children learn, grow, and develop into responsible adults. Discipline is a means to that end and Consequences is a method of disciplining that focuses on learning, growth, and developing responsibility. Punishment is the tool of parents who want to show their superiority and power over their children. Rewards are the tool of parents who want quick and easy compliance.

Which kind of parent are you? I sincerely hope your efforts to use consequences will place you squarely in the first category.

Post-Test

The following test is identical to the pretest you took at the beginning of Lesson II. After you have finished, score both your pre- and post-tests using the answer sheet on page 63. Compare your tests.

What did you learn? Did any of your opinions or ideas change?

True or False:

1. Children can learn to accept responsibility for their own actions.   T   F
2. To discipline a child effectively a certain amount of punishment must be used.   T   F
3. Even preverbal children can learn to understand that their actions have consequences.   T   F
4. Children must learn that parents are older and wiser, so it's all right to say, "I told you so."   T   F
5. Using candy and toys to coax a child to behave may not be the best way to control him, but it has no long-range negative effect.   T   F
6. Just your tone of voice can change a consequence into a punishment.   T   F
7. The child who is constantly bribed to behave would most likely ask which question(s) before deciding to take an action:
    a. How will this help me get ahead?   T   F
    b. How will this help me grow and develop?   T   F
    c. What's in it for me?   T   F
    d. How will this help someone else?   T   F
8. A child should never be given an allowance.   T   F
9. A consequence is that event which is either the natural, logical or prearranged result of the event preceding it.   T   F
10. A child's good behavior should have its roots in his desire to please, belong, cooperate, and contribute.   T   F
11. Punishment is something the parent does *to* the child which emphasizes the parent's personal power and superiority.   T   F
12. To discipline a child means to teach him to behave acceptably.   T   F

Answers to Pretest and Post-Test

1. T
2. F
3. T
4. F
5. F
6. T
7. a. F b. F c. T d. F
8. F
9. T
10. T
11. T
12. T

LESSON III:

REALITY BEHAVIOR TRAINING (R B T)

Children Governing Themselves

Pretest

Please take the following test, circling *T* if you think the statement is true and *F*, if you think it is false. After you have completed this lesson, you will take the test again. By comparing your two test results against the answer key, you will see how much you have learned and in what way your opinions have changed.

1. Children should always be allowed to find their own solutions to their problems.   T   F

2. If my child says he will do something, I do not have to follow up to be sure he did it.   T   F

3. If I checked up on my child, I would feel that I was not trusting him.   T   F

4. My teen-ager knows what will happen to him if he does something wrong.   T   F

5. There is nothing wrong with the following exchange:
   FATHER: You know what you did was wrong, don't you?
   CHILD: Yes.   T   F

6. It is a good idea always to ask your child to explain why he did what he did.   T   F

7. If your child fails to change his behavior after a number of attempts, it is usually because he does not want to change.   T   F

8. Every child wants to love and be loved, no matter how disobedient or mean.   T   F

9. A positive relationship is not essential to teaching your child responsible behavior.   T   F

10. The best time to solve a child's behavior problem is as soon as it is noticeable.   T   F

Situation

Mrs. Brown and her 15-year-old daughter, Karen have a problem. Karen told Mom that she was going to spend the evening at a friend's house. Instead, she secretly met with an older boy that her parents don't like. A neighbor, seeing Karen in the boy's company at a late hour, informed Karen's parents of her true whereabouts.

When Karen returns home, her mother confronts her with this information. Karen is scared, defensive, and hostile. She replies angrily to her mother's questions. Mrs. Brown is angry, hurt, and worried. The scene is set for a terrible fight.

Can you see any way that Karen and Mom could work through this serious problem without having a fight? Is a battle inevitable? In the space below, write what you would do if you were the mother. Then turn to page 66 for a discussion of the possibilities.

We hope that some of you suggested Mom could begin by using Reflective Communication. Both parent and child are upset. If they are going to talk this thing through, they must first calm down.

Mom could say:

"You are angry that I know about last night"

or

"You're really scared about what will happen now"

or

"You must think we don't trust you and that's why we asked you not to see Frank."

There are many ways Mom could open the door to an earnest discussion. You may have thought of even better responses than those mentioned.

Some of you may have suggested using Consequences to discipline Karen.

Let's consider the use of logical consequences. If Karen continues to see an older boy in the late evening, she could become sexually involved with him and have either a devastating emotional experience or a baby! Certainly, these are not acceptable consequences and Mom would not want Karen to suffer them, no matter how well she would learn her lesson. A more acceptable consequence of Karen's behavior might be restriction. If Karen cannot be trusted to go to a friend's house when she says that is where she is going, then Karen cannot go out unsupervised for a set period of time. There is a logical connection between lying about where you are going and not being allowed to go out at all.

If you thought of using Reflective Communication and Consequences, good for you! In dealing with Karen's problem, both techniques could be useful; however, for a child Karen's age and a problem this serious, you're probably wishing there was something more. Reality Behavior Training (RBT) provides you with something more.

What Is Reality Behavior Training?

Reality Behavior Training is a detailed guide to solving problems. As parent and child use RBT, the child learns to:

1. Evaluate his decisions and actions
2. Foresee consequences
3. Arrive at realistic plans to solve his problems
4. Deal responsibly with reality

RBT is Lesson III in this workbook because it builds on the techniques discussed in Lessons I and II. To use RBT, you will need the help of Reflective Communication and Consequences because RBT is effective only when:

1. The general parent-child relationship is good
2. The situation is calm
3. The child understands that his actions have consequences for which he is responsible

An Outline of RBT's Basic Steps

Prerequisite:

Because the child must cooperate in the RBT process, it is important that you have established a basically good relationship with your child. We hope your use of reflective communication in the past two weeks has helped to strengthen your relationship.

Four steps make up the RBT process:

Step One: *The child identifies his behavior.*

Step Two: *The child makes a value judgement of his behavior*
and/or

Step Three: *The child identifies the consequences of his behavior and makes a value judgement of them.*

Step Four: *The child formulates a plan and makes a commitment to follow it.*

Before going on, let's expand these four steps just a little.

Step One: The child identifies his own inappropriate behavior. The child, not the parent, must state what the child is doing wrong.

Step Two: The child makes a value judgement *not* the parent.

Step Three: The child must identify the consequences of his actions. If the parent points out the consequences, he will not be sure that the child believes these consequences will really result.

Step Four: The child formulates a plan. This plan should aim to eliminate the inappropriate behavior and make amends where necessary. It is helpful if the plan contains specifics: what, where, and when. The parent can offer help in a supportive manner. Should the child fail to implement his plan, both parent and child are committed to reformulate the plan together and try again.

As you can see, RBT requires the child's cooperation. But why, you are probably asking yourself, should my child wish to cooperate in this kind of procedure. What could motivate him to identify his own inappropriate behavior, make value judgements, and formulate plans?

Four
Basic
Needs
of All
Children

If psychologists agree on anything, it is that human beings have four basic needs:

1. To be loved
2. To love
3. To feel worthwhile to others
4. To feel worthwhile to themselves.

Your child loves you and wants to please you. He wants you to love him in return. He also needs to feel his own worth. RBT will help your child see that he is capable of solving his own problems. And as he overcomes them, he will begin to feel more valuable as a member of the family, a person of worth to himself and to others.

RBT
Corollaries

There are three corollaries to the four RBT steps, which are important to remember at all times. Think of them as "red flags," warning you when you are treading on dangerous ground.
1. NEVER accept excuses.
2. NEVER punish the child. Let him suffer the consequences of his own actions when possible.
3. NEVER give up on your child. When you give up on him, he gives up on himself.

The RBT steps are simple to list, but more difficult to implement. For this reason, please follow the subsequent directions carefully. RBT will be a valuable tool if you learn to use it properly.

Now please turn to page 70.

Ooooops! You didn't follow the instructions. Nowhere in this lesson are you directed to turn to this page. So go back to page 68 and be sure to follow the instructions carefully as you progress through the lesson.

BETTER PARENTS, BETTER CHILDREN

Please read the following dialogue. It is an example of RBT in action.

A father watched his eight-year-old son steal some cherries from a neighbor's yard.

DAD:	Bob, what do you have in your pocket?
BOB:	Just some cherries.
DAD:	Where did you get the cherries?
BOB:	Down in Mr. Miller's orchard.
DAD:	Did he give them to you?
BOB:	No.
DAD:	How did you get them?
BOB:	Well, I sort of took them.
DAD:	What do we call that, son?
BOB:	I guess it's kind of stealing. (CHILD IDENTIFIES BEHAVIOR.)
DAD:	Is that what you are supposed to do?
BOB:	No. (CHILD MAKES VALUE JUDGEMENT OF BEHAVIOR.)
DAD:	What happens when boys take things that don't belong to them?
BOB:	They get in trouble. (CHILD IDENTIFIES CONSEQUENCES.)
DAD:	What else?
BOB:	People get angry at them and then they don't trust them anymore.
DAD:	Is that what you want, Bob?
BOB:	No. (CHILD MAKES VALUE JUDGEMENT OF CONSEQUENCES.)
DAD:	What do you think you could do?
BOB:	Not steal any more cherries. (CHILD BEGINS TO FORMULATE PLAN.)
DAD:	What about the ones in your pocket?
BOB:	I guess I should take them back.
DAD:	Is that all?
BOB:	I could throw them over the fence.
DAD:	Would that make it right?
BOB:	No.
DAD:	Well then, what else could you do?
BOB:	I guess I ought to give them back and say I'm sorry. (CHILD CONTINUES TO FORMULATE PLAN.)
DAD:	That's a good idea. When can you do it?
BOB:	I guess I could do it now. (CHILD MAKES COMMITMENT.)
DAD:	Is there any way I can help?
BOB:	Sort of. I'm afraid of Mr. Miller. Will you go with me and just be there beside me?
DAD:	Of course, son. Let's go.

There are several basic assumptions underlying RBT. One of these is that a child cannot change his past behavior. Therefore, RBT concerns itself only with present and future behavior. (By present, we include also incidences of the behavior that closely precede the RBT session.) If you have an RBT session with your child on Wednesday, which of the following behaviors would you be able to change?

    _____A.   Breaking a window the previous Monday. (If this is the correct response, turn to page 72 .)

    _____B.   Planning to skip school Thursday. (If this is the correct response, turn to page 73 .)

You said that on Wednesday the child would be able to change the unacceptable behavior of the previous Monday. Undoubtedly, he could make amends for the act and should do so. But the act, itself, is history; it has already occurred and can never be erased or changed in any way.

Go back to page 71 and reread the alternate response.

You said that on Wednesday the child could change his unacceptable plan to skip school on Thursday and you're right. Only present behavior or future intentions can be changed. Therefore, logically, the child can be asked to change only them.

Another principle of RBT is that it deals just with reality—i.e., circumstances and events as they really exist, not as they were, should have been, or ideally ought to be (except as the child can change them). This forms the basis for another principle of RBT: The child is responsible for his own behavior and must accept the consequences of it, whatever they may be. Whether or not the consequences are justified or reasonable is not a matter for concern here. The reality is that certain consequences result from certain behavior. These are facts of life. If a child desires different consequences, he must change his behavior to get the results he wants.

At this point, then, let's review the four steps in RBT.

1. The child (NOT the parent) must identify his behavior. Both must be sure they are talking about the same behavior. If the child identifies his own behavior, there is no question as to what he thinks he is doing. Which of the following dialogues achieves the first step of RBT?

————A.

PARENT: Why did you steal the money from my purse?
JOE: I didn't steal it.

Turn to page 75 if you think this dialogue is correct.

————B.

PARENT: Joe, why did you take the money from my purse?
JOE: I just was going to borrow it. I would have put it back.

Turn to page 76 if you think this dialogue is correct.

————C.

PARENT: Joe, where did you get that money?
JOE: From your purse.
PARENT: What is that called when you take without permission?
JOE: Stealing.

Turn to page 77 if you think this dialogue is correct.

Incorrect. Remember: It is essential that the child identify his own behavior. In this dialogue, the parent has already decided that Joe stole the money and accuses him of that behavior. Joe's reply indicates that **he** doesn't think he did what the **parent** thinks he did. Even if Joe took the money, if he doesn't think he was stealing, he will refuse to accept responsibility for the act. As long as the conversation is about what the parent thinks instead of what Joe thinks, you can be sure that Joe will feel the conversation has little relevance to him, no matter how stern the lecture. Remember, the child must identify his own behavior.

Please turn back to page 74 and select a more appropriate response.

Incorrect. Even though the parent did not use the word steal and asked the question with more love and respect, it was still the parent who identified the behavior first. This approach is awkward and can be threatening to a child. When the parent's and Joe's statements are taken together, it can be seen readily that the child identified his own behavior primarily in self-defense. He did not initiate the identification on his own.

Go back to page 74   Re-study your response, and then make another selection.

Correct. You observed that the parent motivated the child to identify his own behavior. This is the first step of RBT.

Go on to the next page.

BETTER PARENTS, BETTER CHILDREN

If the child does not identify his behavior correctly or deliberately avoids identifying it because he knows what you want him to say, keep asking, "What else are you doing?" until he arrives at the correct response.

Once the child has identified his behavior, most parents will naturally tend to ask, "Why?" DON'T!! Don't ask for excuses. Remember, the child is responsible for his behavior. No matter how good a child's reasons are for doing an unacceptable act, the fact is that he still did the act and the reality of life is that he will experience the consequences of that act no matter how good his excuse for doing it. Therefore, don't invite excuses by asking "Why?" If excuses are volunteered, don't accept them as a justification for unacceptable behavior.

Which of the following dialogues illustrates correct handling of excuses?

—————A.

PARENT: What happened this morning when you went to school?
BETTE: I didn't make it on time.
PARENT: Is this the first time?
BETTE: No, I guess I've been late a lot this year. But I have to wait for Kathy at the corner so we can walk together. She's new in school this year and she doesn't have many friends. Some of the other girls are mean to her, so I walk with her to be friendly. She's late a lot, so I've been late a lot too.
PARENT: Oh Bette, I didn't know. That's very kind of you. But please, do the best you can to be on time from now on.

If you think this dialogue illustrates the correct handling of excuses, turn to page 79 .

—————B.

PARENT: What happened this morning when you went to school?
BETTE: I didn't make it on time.
PARENT: Why didn't you?
BETTE: I had to wait for Kathy at the corner so we could walk together. She's new in school this year. Some of the other girls aren't nice to her, so I walk with her to be friendly. She's late a lot, so I've been late a lot.
PARENT: That's all very nice, Bette, but if you continue to be late to class you'll fall behind in your work and your teacher will be upset with you.

If you think this dialogue illustrates the correct handling of excuses, turn to page 80 .

—————C.

PARENT: What happened this morning when you went to school?
BETTE: I didn't make it on time.
PARENT: Is this the first time?
BETTE: No, I guess I've been late a lot this year. But I have to wait for Kathy at the corner so we can walk together. She's new in school this year and she doesn't have many friends. Some of the other girls aren't nice to her, so I walk with her to be friendly. She's late a lot so I've been late a lot too.
PARENT: What happens when you keep coming to class late?
BETTE: I guess the teacher doesn't like it. She gets angry.
PARENT: What else?
BETTE: I miss some classwork and fall behind.

If you think this dialogue illustrates the correct handling of excuses, turn to page 81 .

Ah, come on now. Don't let your heart rule your head. The excuse seems valid and the parent's response is warm and friendly, but the reality is that Bette will continue to arrive late and will get even further behind in her classwork. Accepting her excuse does not help her at all.

Go back to page 78 and select another response.

Dialogue B is incorrect. By asking Bette why she was late, the parent invites her to make excuses. Then, the parent identifies the consequences of being late, leaving Bette out of the problem-solving process.

Go back to page 78 and select another response.

Right you are. Dialogue C is correct. Even though the excuse seems to be valid, the reality is that Bette cannot continue coming late to school and still succeed with her classwork. In Dialogue C, the parent does not allow Bette's excuses to sidetrack the RBT process. Instead, the parent guides Bette to identify her behavior and the consequences of her action.

Turn to the next page.

Once the child has identified his behavior, the parent may choose *either* or *both* of two alternatives in following the RBT process.

1. He may lead the child to make a value judgement of his act. For example, if a child says he is stealing, the parent might ask, "Is that right?" or "Does it make you feel good?"

and/or

2. The parent may lead the child to identify the consequences of his act. For example, the parent may ask, "What happens to people who steal?" If the child accurately identifies the consequences of his act, the parent then leads him to make a value judgement of those consequences: "Is that what you want?"

The choice may be illustrated as follows:

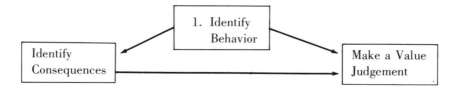

In other words, you may either

Identify the Behavior		Identify the Behavior
Make a Value Judgement of the Behavior	or	Identify the Consequences
		Make a Value Judgement of the Consequences.

If you try one path first and arrive at a dead end, then you can back up and try the alternate path.

For example:

PARENT: What is that called?

CHILD: I guess it's stealing. (Child identifies behavior.)

PARENT: Is that a good thing to do? (Parent invites value judgement of the behavior.)

CHILD: I don't know; it doesn't bother me. They're really rich; they can afford it. (Child makes value judgement.)

DEAD END

Alternate Path:

PARENT: What happens to people who steal?

CHILD: They get in trouble. (Child identifies consequence of behavior.)

PARENT: Yes, what else?

CHILD: Nobody trusts them.

PARENT: Yes, anything else?

CHILD: If they're grown up, they go to jail.

PARENT: That's true. Are these things you want to happen to you? (Parent invites value judgement of the consequences.)

CHILD: No, I guess not. (Child makes value judgement of consequences.)

In which of the following dialogues is the child asked to make a value judgement of his act?

_____A.

JOHNNY: I was drawing on the wall.
PARENT: Is it right to draw on the wall?
JOHNNY: No, I guess not.

If this is correct, then turn to page 84.

_____B.

JOHNNY: I was drawing on the wall.
PARENT: Why were you doing that?
JOHNNY: Because I wanted to draw you a pretty picture. I looked for paper, but there wasn't any.

If this is correct, turn to page 85.

Good work. You correctly identified that Johnny was asked to make a value judgement of his act when the parent asked him if drawing on the wall was all right.

Turn to page 86.

Isn't that sweet! He wants to please mother. Unfortunately, the mother was completely incorrect in her use of RBT. She not only did *not* ask him to make a value judgement of his behavior, but she violated another principle by asking for an excuse. She asked "Why!" And he came up with a lulu. See how excuses foul things up?

Turn back to page 83 and re-read the other answer.

Which of the following dialogues leads the child to identify the consequences of his behavior?

_____A.

CHILD: I'm going to hit my crummy teacher. I hate her.
PARENT: What do you think will happen then?
CHILD: They'll probably throw me out of school.

If this is correct, turn to page 88.

_____B.

CHILD: I'm going to hit my crummy teacher. I hate her.
PARENT: I guess you know that you'll be kicked out of school.
CHILD: Yep. And I don't care.

If this is correct, turn to page 87.

Afraid not. A consequence is identified, but not by the child. Remember: The child should identify the consequences of his behavior when he can. The parent may have to identify some consequences for the child when the child is unaware of them; however, whenever the parent does so, he runs the risk that the child will disagree with his appraisal of the consequences of the behavior.

Return to page 86 and read the alternate answer.

Example A is exactly right. The child is led to identify the consequences of his behavior.

Please turn to the next page.

In which of the following dialogues is the child helped to make a value judgement of the consequences of his behavior?

_____A.

PARENT: What happens when you steal?
CHILD: You have to go to juvenile court.
PARENT: Is that what you want?
CHILD: No.

Turn to page 91 if this is correct.

_____B.

PARENT: What do other people think of you when you steal?
MARY: They can't trust you.
PARENT: That's true, Mary, and I'm sure you don't want to become the type of person that cannot be trusted. What can you do to prevent this from happening?
MARY: I can stop taking things that don't belong to me.

Turn to page 90 if this is correct.

A value judgement of the consequences was made, all right, but *not* by the child. The parent was the one who decided that the consequences were bad. While in this case the child may have agreed with the parent, in another the child may actually want the consequences of an unacceptable act. He may, for example, like being left home. As long as the child desires the consequences of his actions, it is futile to expect him to change his behavior, even if everyone else in the entire world thinks the consequences are bad. Therefore, the child himself should be led to make a value judgement of the consequences of his behavior.

Go back to page 89 and re-read the alternate answer.

You're right. The child made a value judgement of the consequences of his actions when he decided that he did not want to go to juvenile court.

Helpful
Hint

If a child says he doesn't care about a consequence, keep asking, "What else?"

For example:

PARENT: What happens when you steal?

CHILD: You have to go to juvenile court, but I don't care. All they do is slap your wrist.

PARENT: What else happens?

CHILD: I guess I'd get a record.

PARENT: What else?

CHILD: I guess some of the kids wouldn't hang around with me anymore.

PARENT: What else?

CHILD: I guess you and Dad would be pretty angry at me.

PARENT: We'd feel terrible, that's true. Can you think of anything else?

CHILD: If you get caught a couple of times, they could send you to the state training school.

PARENT: That's true. Are these things you want to happen?.

The idea is to let the list of consequences pile up so that it is ridiculous for the child to say he doesn't care about the consequences.

Once the child has identified his unacceptable behavior and made a value judgement of it and/or the resulting consequences, he is ready for RBT Step Four: to formulate a plan for changing his behavior.

An intrinsic part of the plan should be the child's commitment to it. He should verbalize specifically what he intends to do and, if appropriate, when and/or where.

For example:

PARENT: When can you turn in that late assignment?

CHILD: By Wednesday.

PARENT: Which plan do you want to follow?

CHILD: I won't tease Jerry anymore.

It is essential that the parent be subjective and personal throughout RBT. The child must be able to see that you sincerely want to help him. He should sense your concern in your manner of dealing with him. When the child begins to formulate his plan for changing his behavior, he must know that you are willing to help him in any way you can.

Before a specific plan for change is decided on, the child should be encouraged to suggest and consider possible alternatives. The dialogue might go something like this:

PARENT: Is stealing cherries right?
JOHNNY: No.
PARENT: What could you do about what you've done?
JOHNNY: Well, I could take the cherries back.
PARENT: Yes, you could. What else?
JOHNNY: I could pay Mr. Brown for the cherries.
PARENT: Yes, you could. What else?
JOHNNY: I could apologize to Mr. Brown.
PARENT: Yes, what else?
JOHNNY: I could make sure I never steal again.
PARENT: Yes, you could. And what else?
JOHNNY: You could go with me to talk to Mr. Brown.
PARENT: Yes, I could. What else?
JOHNNY: You could take the cherries back to Mr. Brown.
PARENT: Yes. What else?
JOHNNY: I could call Mr. Brown and tell him what I've done.
PARENT: Yes, you could. What else?

From the group of alternative plans he has suggested, the child should select one or more which he feels are best and which he will follow. Together, he and the parent then decide on the details of how he will follow the plan.

If the child cannot think of any possible plans or any that are acceptable, the parent may suggest some possibilities. If the child wants to follow a plan that the parent considers unacceptable, the parent should honestly, forthrightly, and sincerely tell him that the alternative is not acceptable and he should select another one.

Here is another example of the fourth step of RBT, this time proceeding from a value judgement of consequences instead of a value judgement of the act:

PARENT: What will happen when you turn in only 2 of the 16 major assignments for the term?
JOHNNY: I guess they'll flunk me and I won't be able to graduate.
PARENT: Is that what you want?
JOHNNY: No, I sure don't.
PARENT: What do you want?
JOHNNY: I want to get a passing grade and graduate.
PARENT: What are some ways you could do that?
JOHNNY: Well, I could work extra hard and do the other 14 assignments. But we only have two weeks left and I don't think I could catch up.
PARENT: Okay. What else?
JOHNNY: Well, they might give me a "D" instead of an "F" so I could graduate.
PARENT: Yes, they could. What else?
JOHNNY: Gee, I can't think of any other ways.
PARENT: Well, you could do part of the work and raise your grade to at least passing.
JOHNNY: Yes, I guess I could.
PARENT: You might do some special assignments and earn enough credit to pass.
JOHNNY: Yeah, I could do that.

PARENT: Which of these would be the best way for you to get a passing grade and graduate, as you would like?

JOHNNY: Well, I could talk to them about giving me a "D" instead of an "F" and letting me graduate anyway.

PARENT: No, Johnny. I'm sorry, but the plan is unacceptable.

JOHNNY: Well, could I talk to them about doing part of the work in the time I have left and salvaging part of my grade?

PARENT: That would be fine, Johnny. How much do you think you could do in the two weeks left?

JOHNNY: Well, I guess I could do four more of the assignments. That should be enough to get me a "D."

PARENT: Do you know that four assignments will do it?

JOHNNY: No, but I will check tomorrow morning with my teacher.

PARENT: Good, and if it is all right with your teacher, when will you turn in the first assignment?

JOHNNY: I don't know. It seems that I just don't have time to do very much homework after I finish everything else that I have to do at night. Besides, I don't understand the assignments very well.

PARENT: Do you think you can spend one hour each night on these assignments?

JOHNNY: I guess so.

PARENT: Good. If you'll promise me you'll spend an hour every night on these assignments, I'll make myself available whenever you need help, okay?

JOHNNY: Okay. Thanks. If this is all okay with my teacher, I'll try to get the first assignment in on Wednesday.

PARENT: Fine.

When the child does better in school, he will feel better. And, he is more likely to follow a plan he has helped to outline. If, however, he does not follow the plan, the parent should have another session with him in which the child re-commits himself to the plan, chooses another alternative from his previous list, or formulates a new plan.

A
Short
Review

Once again, the four steps of RBT are:

1. Child identifies his behavior.
2. Child makes a value judgement of his behavior
and/or
3. Child identifies the consequences of his behavior and makes a value judgement of them.
4. Child formulates a plan and makes a commitment to follow it.

Let's see if you can use RBT now, referring only to the above summary of the process. Here is the situation:

Your family has a rule that nobody comes to breakfast before he washes his hands and face and combs his hair. Your daughter, Mary, comes to breakfast every day without first taking care of these details. You have to argue with her every morning before she will go back upstairs to wash and comb her hair. Today, as usual, Mary broke the family rule. What will your first statement or question to her be?

PARENT:

You should have led Mary to *identify her own behavior* (RBT Step One). For example, you could have asked, "What are you doing?" and Mary may have replied, "Getting ready to eat."

What would you say next?

PARENT:

Because Mary did not identify the behavior you were interested in talking about, you should have persevered in getting her to identify that behavior. You might have asked, "Have you missed doing anything this morning?" Actually, a simple "What else?" or "What kind of condition are you in?" would probably do the job. Then, Mary might reply, "I didn't get cleaned up."

We hope you recognize that you have two alternatives at this point and you can choose either one or both. If you choose to have Mary make a value judgement of her behavior, turn to page 98 as soon as you fill in your next response. If, on the other hand, you choose to have her identify the consequences of her behavior, turn to page 100 as soon as you fill in your next reply.

PARENT:

This is how your dialogue might have progressed: (We hope you didn't ask Mary for an excuse!)

PARENT: What are you doing?

MARY: Getting ready to eat.

PARENT: Have you forgotten to do anything this morning?

MARY: I didn't get cleaned up.

→ PARENT: Is it all right in our home to come to the table without washing your face and combing your hair?

MARY: No, but I don't see why we always have to wash first. It doesn't hurt anybody if we don't, does it?

PARENT:

Turn to the next page.

Mary has now made a value judgment, just as you asked her to. She has judged her behavior to be right. As long as she feels this way, she will not change her behavior. Why should she? She thinks she's right. Therefore, it is futile to pursue this avenue. If you fell into the trap of responding directly to Mary's question, the RBT session will probably become sidetracked into an argument:

MARY: No, but I don't see why we always have to wash first. It doesn't hurt anybody if we don't, does it?

PARENT: It bothers me for one, Mary.

MARY: So, it bothers me to have to wash up and comb my hair before I've eaten something.

PARENT: It's unpleasant to sit at the breakfast table with someone who looks a mess!

MARY: It's unpleasant for me to have to wash before I've had my juice!

PARENT: Don't be silly.

MARY: You're the one being silly.

fight

If Mary had judged her behavior to be wrong, you could have gone directly on to RBT Step 4 (formulate a plan to change the behavior). Since she did not, you should have tried to get her to identify the consequences of her behavior.

Turn to page 100

Your question/statement should lead Mary to identify a consequence of her action:

MARY: No, but I don't see why we always have to wash first. It doesn't hurt anybody if we don't, does it?

⟶ PARENT: (Pause for a moment and let the question clear.) What happens when you come downstairs and you are not cleaned up?

MARY: You throw a fit and yell at me.

PARENT:

Turn to the next page.

We hope you didn't let this answer throw you. Mary is trying to engage you in an argument. Don't be pulled off the track. Just keep the dialogue going until you get what you want.

PARENT: What happens when you come downstairs and aren't cleaned up?
MARY: You throw a fit and yell at me.
→ PARENT: What else?
MARY: Well, I don't get to eat breakfast.
PARENT:

You may have wanted to pursue other consequences, but since not getting breakfast is probably a consequence Mary does not want, you might ask her to make a value judgment of this consequence.

CHILD: Well, I don't get to eat breakfast.
PARENT: Is that what you want?
CHILD: No.
PARENT:

Once Mary evaluates the consequences of her behavior, you are ready to go on to the fourth step of RBT: formulation of a plan. Your next question should therefore lead the child to formulate a plan that will change her behavior.

→ PARENT: What are some of the things you can do to prevent your missing breakfast?

CHILD: I could eat in my room where nobody would see me.

PARENT: What else might you do?

CHILD: I could try to get the rule changed.

PARENT: You could. What else?

CHILD: I could get up a little earlier so I could clean myself up in time for breakfast.

PARENT: Yes, what else?

CHILD: I can't think of anything else.

PARENT:

There might have been some additional plans that Mary did not mention. But, she did come up with at least one good one, so you probably should have gone ahead and asked her to select one of the plans. (If she selects a plan that is completely objectionable to you, then let her know that the plan is not acceptable.) Your next statement/question should have been something like this:

MARY: I can't think of anything else.

→ PARENT: All right. Which of the plans do you think would be best for you?

MARY: I think I'll get up earlier.

PARENT: Good. Is there any way I can help?

MARY: Yes, I don't have an alarm clock and I think it would help a lot.

PARENT: I've got an extra one that your Dad uses on trips. You can have it.

MARY: Thanks, Mom.

PARENT:

Your next statement/question should have encouraged Mary to make a commitment to the plan she formulated.

> MARY: Thanks Mom.
> → PARENT: You're welcome. Now, when do you plan to start using the alarm clock?
> MARY: How about tonight?
> PARENT: That's great!

Congratulations! If you've made it this far, chances are that *you* can now use RBT.

Of course, you need practice and the next section of Lesson III will encourage you to do just that.

It might also be a good idea for you to turn back to page 95 and read straight through to this page. The discussion of answers you did not select the first time through will provide you with more information about RBT.

A Complete RBT Dialogue

Here is the complete RBT session that you just constructed piece by piece. Read through it a few times and get a feeling for the RBT pattern. Read through the dialogue with your spouse or a friend. (Maybe you'd like to write out the dialogue using the phrases you inserted and then practice it that way.)

PARENT: What are you doing?

MARY: Getting ready to eat.

PARENT: Have you forgotten to do anything this morning?

MARY: I didn't get cleaned up.

PARENT: Is it all right in our home to come to the table without washing your face and combing your hair?

MARY: No, but I don't see why we always have to wash first. It doesn't hurt anybody if we don't, does it?

PARENT: (after a pause to let the question clear) What happens when you come downstairs and you are not cleaned up?

MARY: Well, I don't get to eat breakfast.

PARENT: Is that what you want?

MARY: No.

PARENT: What are some things that you could do to prevent your missing breakfast?

MARY: I could eat in my room where nobody would see me.

PARENT: What else might you do?

MARY: I could try to get the rule changed.

PARENT: You could. What else?

MARY: I could get up a little earlier so I could clean myself up in time for breakfast.

PARENT: Yes. What else?

MARY: I can't think of anything else.

PARENT: All right. Which of the plans do you think would be best for you?

MARY: I think I'll get up earlier.

PARENT: Good! Is there any way I can help?

MARY: Yes. I don't have an alarm clock and I think it would help a lot.

PARENT: I've got an extra one your Dad uses on trips. You can have it.

MARY: Thanks, Mom.

PARENT: You're welcome. Now, when do you plan to start using the alarm clock?

MARY: How about tonight?

PARENT: That's great!

Did you practice the dialogue with someone else? If not, did you read it out loud? Repeating typical RBT phrases aloud will give you the confidence you need to try the method with your child.

One mother reported that she found it useful to think of RBT in terms of phrases, rather than steps. She broke the procedure down as follows:

What are you doing?
    What else?
    What else?

Is that all right?

What will happen if you continue?
    What else?
    What else?
    What else?

Is that what you want?

What can you do about it?

RBT and Little Children

In its complete form, RBT can be too much for children under the age of five. While most can handle the steps individually, they cannot concentrate on a problem long enough to stay with you throughout an entire RBT procedure. For example: If you ask a four-year-old what he was doing, he could answer, "I was hitting Herbert." If you ask him if hitting is a nice thing to do, he could make a value judgement. The child could answer if you ask him what happens to boys who hit and he could tell you whether he'd want that to happen to him. He could formulate a plan to help him avoid hitting Herbert again and he could make a commitment to that plan. *But* it would be hard for him to do *all* of these things in rapid succession without becoming confused.

Nevertheless, there are lessons to be learned from each individual step of RBT as well as from the whole procedure. For different age groups, you should concentrate on different parts of RBT.

A verbal two-year-old will gladly identify a problem. If asked, "Martha, where are your clothes?," she will answer, "I took them off, Mommy." You will then have to make a value judgement of the action and explain to Martha why the action is right or wrong. Still, identifying the problem herself has helped Martha focus her attention on what you are talking about.

A three-year-old can identify consequences. If you confront Jerry with having drawn on the walls and ask him, "What will happen to you and your crayons now?," Jerry is capable of responding, "You will take away my crayons and I'll have to go to my room."

A four-year-old is capable of imagining a variety of alternative plans. You can say, "Brent, you keep hitting Eric. Hitting is not nice. Now, I want you to sit here and think of some things you can do so you will stop hitting. Then come and tell me your plan." Brent is more likely to follow a plan of his own and you are giving him valuable training in problem solving.

When you think your child is ready to handle all the RBT steps together, give it a try. If he can, terrific! If he can't, then go back to using the different steps at different times and try the complete RBT process again later.

A Final Word

RBT is an effective problem-solving technique. It will help you and your child work through problems together and arrive at solutions that will change his unacceptable behavior.

RBT trains your child to define problems, consider consequences, map out alternative solutions, and formulate plans. This training is good, not just for solving behavioral problems, but for solving all problems!

An RBT session proves to your child that you are concerned about him, that you care enough to take the time to sit down and discuss alternate solutions and formulate plans. The child sees that you are supportive and will help him in any way you can.

Remember the third corollary stated near the beginning of this lesson? *Never give up on your child.* Don't even insinuate that you are going to give up. The first thing we tell children that we see in counseling is, "No matter what you do, we're not going to stop working with you." They usually don't believe it, but they want to believe it. They hope it is true and so they test us. And as they test us and we remain firm, consistent, fair, and caring, that hope turns into reality for them and they change their lives.

Post-Test

The following test is identical to the pretest you took at the beginning of Lesson III. After you have finished, score both your pre- and post-tests using the key on page 110. Compare your tests. What did you learn? Did any of your ideas or opinions change?

1. Children should always be allowed to find their own solutions to their problems.   T   F

2. If my child says he will do something, I do not have to follow up to be sure he did it.   T   F

3. If I checked up on my child, I would feel that I was not trusting him.   T   F

4. My teen-ager knows what will happen to him if he does something wrong.   T   F

5. There is nothing wrong with the following exchange:
   FATHER: You know what you did was wrong, don't you?
   CHILD: Yes.   T   F

6. It is a good idea always to ask your child to explain why he did what he did.   T   F

7. If your child fails to change his behavior after a number of attempts, it is usually because he does not want to change.   T   F

8. Every child wants to love and be loved, no matter how disobedient or mean.   T   F

9. A positive relationship is not essential to teaching your child responsible behavior.   T   F

10. The best time to solve a child's behavior problem is as soon as it is noticeable.   T   F

Answer Key

1. F
2. F
3. F
4. T
5. F
6. F
7. F
8. T
9. F
10. T

CONCLUSION

You have now completed the *Better Parents, Better Children* workbook. You have learned three child-rearing techniques. In any situation you could use one, two or all three of them. To illustrate this, let's consider one last hypothetical situation.

Allen is six and he is being obnoxious. He and his friend Jack are supposedly playing in the backyard, but Allen is being bossy and refuses to share his toys. For about the fifth time, Allen has Jack in tears.

Consequences
MOM: Allen, since you can't play nicely, you'll have to come inside.
ALLEN: Oh, Mom!
MOM: Please come inside.
ALLEN: (coming in the door) Boy! Why do I have to come inside? That Jack is such a cry baby. I wasn't doing anything. Boy!

Reflective Communication
MOM: You're really angry, aren't you?
ALLEN: Yeah, I want to go back outside.

Reflective Communication
MOM: It would be nice to go outside and play.
ALLEN: Can I go?
MOM: Not right now.
ALLEN: Why not?
MOM: You tell me.
ALLEN: I don't know.

RBT
MOM: What were you doing outside?
ALLEN: Playing.
MOM: What else?

Identify Problem
ALLEN: I guess I was bothering Jack.
MOM: Just bothering?
ALLEN: I was making him cry.
MOM: Is that a good thing to do?

Make a Value Judgement
ALLEN: No, but he's such a cry baby.
MOM: What happens when you make Jack cry?

Identify Consequence
ALLEN: You get really angry.
MOM: What else?
ALLEN: Jack gets angry too.
MOM: Anything else?

Identify Consequence
ALLEN: I guess if Jack got really angry enough he wouldn't play with me anymore.
MOM: Are these things you want to happen?

Make a Value Judgment
ALLEN: No.
MOM: What can you do so that these things don't happen?

Formulate Alternative Plans
ALLEN: Tell Jack I'm sorry.
MOM: What else?
ALLEN: Let him use my dump truck.
MOM: That would be nice. Anything else?
ALLEN: Let him play with my bulldozer and grader.
MOM: Those are all good ideas. What are you going to do?

Final Plan

ALLEN: I'll say I'm sorry and then I'll let him play with my dump truck.

MOM: That sounds like a very good plan. Is there anything I can do to help you?

ALLEN: No, I can do it myself.

MOM: Are you going to do it now?

Commitment

ALLEN: Yes. Right now.

MOM: Okay, then I'll see you later.

Reflective Communication, Consequences, and **Reality Behavior Training** can benefit you and your family greatly . . . if you will use them! Please give the methods a chance to work for you. The hardest part will be to begin. Remember:

1. Relax
2. Be yourself
3. Use your own words
4. Use the methods flexibly and interchangeably

GOOD LUCK!

EXTRA SET OF EXERCISES

Pretest

This pretest will gauge how much you know about reflective communication now. At the end of the lesson, you will take the test again; compare your two sets of responses, and see how much you have learned.

As you take the pretest, please answer truthfully. You are the only one who need see your replies and there is nothing to be gained by responding untruthfully.

Under each child's statement, write how you would normally respond:

Example: 1. CHILD: I surely had a good time at the ball game.
                RESPONSE: I am glad you had a nice time.

2. Look, Dad! I cleaned up my room all by myself.

3. Dad, will you stay with me for a little while before I go to sleep?

4. Susy has such beautiful hair. I try and try to make mine look better, but it doesn't.

5. You're the best Mom in the whole world.

6. I shouldn't have hit Tommy. It was wrong.

7. But, Mom, I don't want my hair in a ponytail. It's my hair anyway.

8. Dad, is this model right? Is it good enough?

9. I want to call Evelyn for a date but . . .

10. My teachers never give me a chance. They seem to get angry at me for no reason at all.

11. I want to button my own coat. I'm big now.

12. Dad, I don't want to make this decision. You make it instead.

13. I don't think I'll ever get over Bill. How could he ever drop me for that Susan Chalmers?

14. Everybody else gets to go to the city alone. You just don't trust me.

15. I surely am glad that you and Dad love me enough to set rules for me. Jody's parents don't and she wishes they did.

16. Mom, you are always telling me what to do.

17. If I want to stay out late, you can't stop me.

18. You didn't treat Janet like this when she was my age.

19. You never listen to me.

20. What I do is my business, not yours.

page 3

Feeling Vocabulary Exercise

Please read each of the following statements and write what **feeling** you think the child is most likely experiencing. There may be many correct answers for each statement. Some replies, however, are probably more accurate than others. On page 12 , you will find the one or more feelings considered most accurate.

Example:	Child's Statement	Child's Feeling
	Daddy, Daddy, I picked up all my toys.	proud, excited

1. No matter how hard I try, I still can't make friends.

2. Tom is younger than I and he can walk to school by himself.

3. I don't like it when you go and leave me here.

4. Why can't we go to the circus for my birthday?

5. Oh, boy! Only two more days 'til my birthday.

6. There's nothing to do and nobody to play with.

7. I can't do this homework. It's too hard for me.

8. I'll get bigger someday, won't I, Mommy?

page 10

115

9. I did a good job.

10. You never listen to me.

11. Playing the piano is dumb. Who can learn all those notes anyway?

12. But I'm not Jill and I can't be like her because I'm me.

13. I don't care if Jane gets a new dress for the dance. Who wants a new dress anyway?

14. It's nice just to be with you.

15. All the kids laughed at me when I tried to read today. I'll never read again.

16. I didn't mean to do it.

17. I don't want to live your kind of life.

18. You never say anything nice to me.

19. Oh Mom, it was absolutely the grossest movie I've ever seen! It really made me sick. I still feel a little shaky.

20. (Crying): I wish I had never been born.

page 11

Feeling Reflection Exercise

You are now ready to formulate some feeling reflections. In this exercise you will be asked to write a reflective response to the child's statement. Write what you perceive the child is feeling, but this time respond in complete sentences. (Hint: You do not always have to use the word "feel" in your replies. If the child says he hates to play the piano and you can tell he is frustrated, your response could be "You're frustrated" or "It can be frustrating at times to learn new music," as well as "You *feel* frustrated.") On page 15 , you will find suggested appropriate responses.

Example:

CHILD: Daddy, Daddy, I picked up all my toys.
RESPONSE: Boy, I'll bet that makes you proud.

1. No matter how hard I try, I still can't make friends.

2. Tom is younger than I and he can walk to school by himself.

3. I don't like it when you go and leave me here.

4. Why can't we go to the circus for my birthday?

5. Oh boy! Only two more days 'til my birthday.

6. There's nothing to do and nobody to play with.

7. I can't do this homework. It's too hard for me.

8. I'll get bigger someday, won't I, Mommy?

page 13

9. I did a good job.

10. You never listen to me.

11. Playing the piano is dumb. Who can learn all those notes anyway?

12. But I'm not Jill and I can't be like her because I'm me..

13. I don't care if Jane gets a new dress for the dance. Who wants a new dress anyway?

14. It's nice just to be with you.

15. All the kids laughed at me when I tried to read today. I'll never read again.

16. I didn't mean to do it.

17. I don't want to live your kind of life.

18. You never say anything nice to me.

19. Oh, Mom, it was absolutely the grossest movie I've ever seen! It really made me sick. I still feel a little shaky.

20. (Crying): I wish I had never been born.

page 14

Thought Reflection Exercise

In this exercise you will be asked to supply a thought reflection in response to the child's statement. Respond in complete sentences and then compare your answers with those on page 22. Remember that your responses need not be exactly like those on page 22, but they should match them in tone and general content.

1. I don't like nursery school.

2. I don't like dogs.

3. Some adults are really crazy.

4. My homeroom teacher is the greatest.

5. I want to be just like you when I grow up.

6. It seems that we always fight around our home. I wish our home was like the Marshall's.

7. Jane got angry at me today. I'll never be her friend again.

page 20

8. I'm in the wrong class. This work is too hard for me.

9. Why can't you be more like Jane's mom?

10. I never get to stay up late like John and Bill.

11. Oh, Mom, I wish you understood me.

12. It's none of your business what I do on my dates.

13. You only think of what's good for you and not what is good for me.

14. You don't trust me.

15. Summer school didn't help one bit. I don't understand chemistry any better at all.

16. I'm going to jog every night and eat nothing but grapefruit for two weeks. I've just got to lose 10 pounds.

page 21

Find and Correct This Mother's Mistakes

In the following dialogue, the mother will miss four opportunities to use reflective communication. Read carefully and write down each mistake Mom makes and what she should have said. Then compare your answers with the discussion that follows.

John is six and his mother has recently come home from the hospital with a new baby, John's first sibling. As mother is giving the baby a careful sponge bath in the kitchen, John stalks into the room. He glares at them both and then stalks out, kicking a chair as he leaves.

MOM: John, come back in here. What do you mean kicking that chair?

SON: The dumb old chair got in my way.

MOM: Well, just push it out of the way next time. . . . John, is something wrong? You look so upset.

SON: I . . . I . . . I . . . I hate that baby!

MOM: Oh John, no! You don't hate the baby. He's your brother.

SON: I do, too. I wish he'd never never come here!

MOM: Now, John dear, these are terrible things to say. People don't hate their brothers. You should be happy he's here. Why, pretty soon he'll be running around and you'll have a playmate all the time.

SON: I don't want to play with him. I want to play with you and Daddy like we did before. I don't want him. Can't we take him back to the hospital?

MOM: Now John, that's enough of that kind of talk. We aren't taking the baby back anywhere. He's staying here. He's part of the family now and Mommy and Daddy love you both very much.

Graduation Exercise

In this final exercise, respond to each of the following statements using reflective communication. Read the child's statement, verbalize a response, and then turn the page to read several correct responses. Assess whether or not you responded with the appropriate phrasing. Reflective communication responses can vary, but yours should contain certain basic elements: concern, attention to the child's feelings or thoughts, and a desire to show your child that you are interested and want to understand him.

1. Look Mom, I got an A on my test in English.

2. Nobody will be my friend.

3. No matter what I do, I just cannot study for this test.

4. We studied Congress in civics today and I think the system stinks.

5. I am afraid to go to the recital and have everybody watch me.

6. What happens if I make a mistake in front of the whole class?

7. It seems that I always want a lot of praise from people.

8. I hate to cry. I always do.

9. Please don't leave me with the babysitter. I don't like it.

10. But everybody does it.

11. Daddy, the kids hurt my feelings.

12. I don't like you anymore.

13. You treat me as if I were 10 years old, but I'm not.

14. I don't know why I did it; I just did it.

15. You don't care what happens to me, only what your precious neighbors will think.

16. You don't love me and you never have.

page 29

Post-Test

Under each child's statement write how you would respond using **Reflective Communication.** Some possible responses are on page 33 . You will want to compare your post-test responses with those you gave on the pretest when you began this course.

1. I surely had a good time at the ball game.

2. Look, Dad. I cleaned up my room all by myself.

3. Dad, will you stay with me for a little while before I go to sleep?

4. Susy has such beautiful hair. I try and try to make mine look better but it doesn't.

5. You're the best Mom in the whole world.

6. I shouldn't have hit Tommy. It was wrong.

7. But Mom, I don't want my hair in a ponytail. It's my hair anyway.

8. Dad, is this model right? Is it good enough?

9. I want to call Evelyn for a date but . . .

page 31

123

10. My teachers never give me a chance. They seem to get angry at me for no reason at all.

11. I want to button my own coat. I'm big now.

12. Dad, I don't want to make this decision. You make it instead.

13. I don't think I'll ever get over Bill. How could he ever drop me for that Susan Chalmers?

14. Everybody else gets to go to the city. You just don't trust me.

15. I sure am glad that you and Dad love me enough to set rules for me. Jody's parents don't and she wishes they did.

16. Mom, you are always telling me what to do.

17. If I want to stay out late, you can't stop me.

18. You didn't treat Janet like this when she was my age.

19. You never listen to me.

20. What I do is my business, not yours.

page 32

124

Pretest

Please take the following test, circling *T* if you think the statement is true and *F*, if you think it is false. Once you have completed the lesson, you will take the test again. By comparing your two sets of responses, you will see how much you have learned and how your opinions have changed.

1. Children can learn to accept responsibility for their own actions.   T   F

2. To discipline a child effectively a certain amount of punishment must be used.   T   F

3. Even preverbal children can learn that their actions have consequences.   T   F

4. Children must learn that parents are older and wiser, so it's all right to say, "I told you so."   T   F

5. Using candy and toys to coax a child to behave may not be the best way to control him, but it has no long-range negative effects.   T   F

6. Just your tone of voice can change a consequence into a punishment.   T   F

7. The child who is constantly bribed to behave would most likely ask which question(s) before deciding to take an action.
   a. How will this help me get ahead?   T   F
   b. How will this help me grow and develop?   T   F
   c. What's in it for me?   T   F
   d. How will this help someone else?   T   F

8. A child should never be given an allowance.   T   F

9. A consequence is that event which is either the natural, logical or prearranged result of the event preceding it.   T   F

10. A child's good behavior should have its roots in his desire to please, belong, cooperate, and contribute.   T   F

11. Punishment is something the parent does *to* the child which emphasizes the parent's personal power and superiority.   T   F

12. To discipline a child means to teach him to behave acceptably.   T   F

page 36

Consequences

Exercise:

See if you can match the following examples to the different kinds of consequences (natural, logical, and prearranged). There are several examples of each kind of consequence.

Place letters here

Natural Consequences _____

Logical Consequences _____

Prearranged Consequences _____

a. If Betsy touches a hot stove, she will be burned.

b. A bike continually left out overnight is likely to get stolen.

c. Mary and her parents have agreed that any belongings left out of place after 9:00 p.m. will be collected and put in a box, not to be removed until the following Monday.

d. If Johnny is still undressed by the time Mom is ready to go out, he will not be able to go with her.

e. A lunchbox left dirty overnight will be smelly and repulsive by morning.

f. If Mom has to clean up Jenny's room in the morning, she will not have time that evening to hem Jenny's new dress for the next day.

g. Children are likely to stub their toes if they play barefoot.

h. Damp clothes left in a heap long enough will mildew.

i. Bobby and his parents agreed that if he failed to clean his hamster's cage once a week, the pet would have to go.

j. A child who refuses to eat dinner and receives no evening snacks will be hungry by breakfast.

page 42

Analysis

Can you complete the analysis of these two examples? Choose words from the list provided and fill in the blanks. All the words should be used, but only once.

In Example #1, Dad acts as an _____ of the rules. He is not _____ Tom. No one is being _____ to Tom. Tom _____ the family rule about Saturday jobs and he has_____ not to do his job. The _____ is that he will not play ball Saturday afternoon until he mows the lawn.

mean
understands
chosen
consequence
punishing
enforcer

In Example #2, Dad _____ Tom. He raises his voice. He calls Tom _____. Dad_____ Tom in a _____ struggle. In Example Two it is not Tom vs. the _____. It is Tom vs. _____. The interaction creates _____ and _____.

rules
power
engages
Dad
resentment
berates
lazy
anger

page 46

Analysis

Can you complete the analysis of these two examples? Choose words from the list provided and fill in the blanks. All the words should be used, but only once.

In Example #1, Mother is_____. Terry a_____. Some parents con themselves into thinking that "_____ you'll clean up your room,_____ I'll let you have a party" is a _____ consequence. But it's not. It is a bribe and contributes to the "_____ _____ _____ _____ _____" philosophy.

what's
if
for
it
then
bribe
offering
prearranged
in
me

page 47

BETTER PARENTS, BETTER CHILDREN

In Example #2, Mother allows a _____ consequence to occur. When a room is not _____ on a regular basis, it becomes_____ to live in. The room is_____. Mom literally closes the door on it. She does not_____and she does not go in.

Eventually Terry will realize that Mom is truly_____. She is ____going to clean up Terry's room. She is not going to_____ Terry to clean up her room. Terry is the only one_____. Nobody else has even mentioned the room for weeks! It becomes_____to Terry that the room is her_____ and_____must keep it neat or _____ the _____.

_____the room has been cleaned, Mom can comment on how nice it looks. But she_____ saying, "It's about_____!"

Terry may also get her_____, but the party and the room are not _____together. The general feeling in the home should be: You _____and you_____, rather than you will be_____with a party for cleaning your room.

discussed
unconcerned
responsibility
cleaned
suffering
Terry's
contribute
natural
after
paid
comment
clear
unpleasant
not
party
suffer
time
bribe
avoids
receive
consequences
she

page 48

Three
Exercises

Exercise I

Try to distinguish between consequences, punishment, and reward by writing C, P or R in the space following each statement. The correct answers are on Page 51.

1. Honestly, Andrew! I told you that pan was still hot. Look at that burn! Why can't you listen? _____

2. Since you can't play with the other children nicely, Ralph, you'll have to come inside. _____

3. If you pick up your toys, Linda, then I'll take you to the park. _____

4. Oh, Andrew, what a nasty burn! I'll bet that hurts. _____

5. I've told you à hundred times not to hit other children! Now, get into this house! _____

6. I warned you that you'd break the doll house by sitting on it, Ann. And don't think I'm going to buy you a new one. _____

7. If you pull three A's this semester, son, I'll get you a car of your own. _____

8. One more smart remark, Miss, and I'll slap your mouth. (Child talks back again; parent slaps child's mouth.) _____

9. I'm sorry your doll house is broken, Ann. _____

10. Patty, I do not have to carry on a conversation with someone who cannot speak nicely. _____

page 50

Exercise II

Study the following examples. In some, the parents have used consequences well. In others, they have made mistakes. In the space provided, write either correct, if you feel the parent has made good use of consequences, or incorrect, if you discern a mistake. If you write incorrect, then underline the sentence or sentences in the example that you think contain an error. When you finish, compare your answers with those on page 54.

Example # 1

Susan is a fussy eater. Tonight, as usual, she is playing with her food. The rest of the family is about finished eating. Susan's family has had a conference. Together they agreed that everyone must eat what is on his dinner plate in order to receive dessert or a snack of any kind later in the evening.

DADDY: (with great patience) Susan, please eat your dinner. If you don't, you'll be hungry. Do you want to be hungry? Remember, if you don't eat, then no dessert or snacks.

SUSAN: I'm not hungry, Daddy.

DADDY: Okay, but remember: no dessert or snacks.

Answer: _____

Example # 2

Toby is five years old. Sick as an infant and toddler, Toby developed an atitude of helplessness. Now well and able to do things for himself, Toby keeps his family in servitude by continuing to appear helpless. One morning Mom lays out Toby's clothes.

MOM: Get dressed dear and then you can go out and play.

TOBY: I can't; you have to help me.

MOM: (pleasantly) I have my own work to do, Toby.

Mom then leaves the room. If Toby attempts to go outside undressed, mother brings him back inside and explains that it it not acceptable for children to play outside undressed. Mom goes about her own business, refusing to be drawn into an argument. She remains firm about the need for Toby to get dressed before he goes outside to play.

Answer: _____

page 52

Example # 3

Jerry is a forgetful 10-year-old. Several times a week Mom must take his lunch to school for him. Mom has pleaded, scolded, and punished, but Jerry still forgets his lunch. One morning Mom decides to use consequences. "Here is your lunch, Jerry," she says calmly. "It is your lunch, not mine. It is your responsibility to take your lunch to school with you each day. If you forget it, I will not bring it to you."

The next day Jerry forgets his lunch again. Mom does *not* take it to school. Without lunch, Jerry gets hungry. (Mom may find it necessary to seek the school's assistance so that Jerry is not given lunch or lunch money.) Jerry is angry when he gets home. "Why didn't you bring me my lunch?" Jerry demands.

"I'm sorry you were hungry, Jerry," Mother replies calmly. "I hope you've learned something from this."

Answer: _____

page 52

Example # 4

Thirteen-year-old Marcy stands on a stool while her mother tries to mark a hem on the dress she is wearing. As usual, Marcy is not being very cooperative. Fitting sessions with Marcy are a hassle for Mom. Today she decides to try consequences.

MOM:	Marcy, please stand still. I can't mark this properly if you don't.
MARCY:	(shifting her weight): It's hard to stand up straight for so long.
MOM:	I know. But if you don't stand straight the marks will all be crooked.
MARCY:	(shifting her weight) It's hard to stand up straight for so long.
MOM:	I know. But if you don't stand straight the marks will all be crooked.
MARCY:	(shifting again) Would you please hurry up, Mom. This is such a drag.
MOM:	(closing her pin book and gathering up her equipment) You can get down now.
MARCY:	But I was going to wear this dress tomorrow.
MOM:	You'll have to find something else.

Answer: _____

page 53

Exercise III

You have now completed several exercises aimed at teaching you to use consequences. Do you think you can do it? Let's see.

You will be presented with a situation and a child's remark. In the space provided, write what you would *say* or *do* in response.

Don't get flustered and go blank. Relax. There are many correct responses. Have you noticed how often reflective communication works well? Sometimes removing the child from a situation he can't handle acceptably is the answer. Sometimes you should withdraw. At times, no response is the right response. And remember how we talked about letting your imagination flow? Try to picture the natural or logical result of your child's action. Is it a consequence you can allow your child to suffer without serious injury occurring? Will your child learn a useful lesson if you allow the consequence to occur? If so, then the consequence is acceptable. Let it happen.

When you have checked your answers with the answer key and made corrections, read through the dialogues with someone else. Reciting the right responses out loud is excellent preparation for using consequences with your child.

Situation # 1

Your two-year-old Megan whines and fusses constantly. She cries at the drop of a hat. She wants her own way and if she doesn't get it she throws a fit. You have tried spanking and scolding; you have been extra patient and loving. You have even tried Reflective Communication. Now you have decided to try Consequences.

PARENT: Want a popsicle, Megan?
MEGAN: I want a red one.
PARENT: There are only purple ones left.
MEGAN: I don't like purple. I want red! Whine, whine, fuss, fuss.
PARENT: _____
MEGAN: Whine, fuss.
PARENT: _____

Situation # 2

You have given four-year-old Ryan all of your odd spoons to use in his sandbox. You caution him that the spoons could be lost easily in the grass if he takes them out of the sandbox. The next day Ryan comes in asking for more spoons.

RYAN: I can't find any of my spoons. May I have some more please?
PARENT: _____
RYAN: But I want more spoons. They're really fun. They make neat shovels. I can dig deep holes. Come on!
PARENT: _____

Situation # 3

Eight-year-old Mike is cleaning fish with a sharp knife. He has your permission to use the knife, but isn't very experienced at cleaning fish. Mike slips and cuts himself.

MIKE: (crying) Ouch! Help, I cut myself.
PARENT: _____

page 55

132

Situation # 4

Eight-year-old Bonnie likes to cook. This is great, but there are several appliances you have asked her not to use without help. The deep fat fryer is one. French fries are planned for tonight and the grease is heating. Bonnie is slicing potatoes and you leave the kitchen for a minute. You hear a shriek and come running back. Bonnie tried dropping potatoes into the fryer and burned herself.

BONNIE: Ouch. Ouch. Ouch. Oh, my hand!

PARENT: _____

_____

(Later, after the burn is cared for)

PARENT: _____

Situation # 5

Your 16-year-old, Ben, has gotten a ticket for speeding:

BEN: It just didn't seem that I was going that fast.

PARENT: _____

Situation # 6

Deb is your family's fussy eater. (Age, if it's over two, doesn't matter here.)

Deb is pushing the food around on her plate. She has been doing that since the meal was served.

PARENT: _____

_____

Deb continues to play with her food.

PARENT: _____

DEB: (the food still on her plate) I'm done. May I be excused?

PARENT: _____

page 56

Post-Test

The following test is identical to the pretest you took at the beginning of Lesson II. After you have finished, score both your pre- and post-tests using the answer sheet on page 63. Compare your tests.

What did you learn? Did any of your opinions or ideas change?

True or False:

1. Children can learn to accept responsibility for their own actions.   T   F
2. To discipline a child effectively a certain amount of punishment must be used.   T   F
3. Even preverbal children can learn to understand that their actions have consequences.   T   F
4. Children must learn that parents are older and wiser, so it's all right to say, "I told you so."   T   F
5. Using candy and toys to coax a child to behave may not be the best way to control him, but it has no long-range negative effect.   T   F
6. Just your tone of voice can change a consequence into a punishment.   T   F
7. The child who is constantly bribed to behave would most likely ask which question(s) before deciding to take an action:
    a. How will this help me get ahead?   T   F
    b. How will this help me grow and develop?   T   F
    c. What's in it for me?   T   F
    d. How will this help someone else?   T   F
8. A child should never be given an allowance.   T   F
9. A consequence is that event which is either the natural, logical or prearranged result of the event preceding it.   T   F
10. A child's good behavior should have its roots in his desire to please, belong, cooperate, and contribute.   T   F
11. Punishment is something the parent does *to* the child which emphasizes the parent's personal power and superiority.   T   F
12. To discipline a child means to teach him to behave acceptably.   T   F

page 62

Pretest

Please take the following test, circling *T* if you think the statement is true and *F*, if you think it is false. After you have completed this lesson, you will take the test again. By comparing your two test results against the answer key, you will see how much you have learned and in what way your opinions have changed.

1. Children should always be allowed to find their own solutions to their problems.   T   F
2. If my child says he will do something, I do not have to follow up to be sure he did it.   T   F
3. If I checked up on my child, I would feel that I was not trusting him.   T   F
4. My teen-ager knows what will happen to him if he does something wrong.   T   F
5. There is nothing wrong with the following exchange:
   FATHER: You know what you did was wrong, don't you?
   CHILD: Yes.   T   F
6. It is a good idea always to ask your child to explain why he did what he did.   T   F
7. If your child fails to change his behavior after a number of attempts, it is usually because he does not want to change.   T   F
8. Every child wants to love and be loved, no matter how disobedient or mean.   T   F
9. A positive relationship is not essential to teaching your child responsible behavior.   T   F
10. The best time to solve a child's behavior problem is as soon as it is noticeable.   T   F

Situation

Mrs. Brown and her 15-year-old daughter, Karen have a problem. Karen told Mom that she was going to spend the evening at a friend's house. Instead, she secretly met with an older boy that her parents don't like. A neighbor, seeing Karen in the boy's company at a late hour, informed Karen's parents of her true whereabouts.

When Karen returns home, her mother confronts her with this information. Karen is scared, defensive, and hostile. She replies angrily to her mother's questions. Mrs. Brown is angry, hurt, and worried. The scene is set for a terrible fight.

Can you see any way that Karen and Mom could work through this serious problem without having a fight? Is a battle inevitable? In the space below, write what you would do if you were the mother. Then turn to page 66 for a discussion of the possibilities.

page 65

There are several basic assumptions underlying RBT. One of these is that a child cannot change his past behavior. Therefore, RBT concerns itself only with present and future behavior. (By present, we include also incidences of the behavior that closely precede the RBT session.) If you have an RBT session with your child on Wednesday, which of the following behaviors would you be able to change?

_____A.   Breaking a window the previous Monday. (If this is the correct response, turn to page 72 .)

_____B.   Planning to skip school Thursday. (If this is the correct response, turn to page 73 .)

page 71

At this point, then, let's review the four steps in RBT.

1. The child (NOT the parent) must identify his behavior. Both must be sure they are talking about the same behavior. If the child identifies his own behavior, there is no question as to what he thinks he is doing. Which of the following dialogues achieves the first step of RBT?

_____A.

PARENT: Why did you steal the money from my purse?

JOE: I didn't steal it.

Turn to page 75 if you think this dialogue is correct.

_____B.

PARENT: Joe, why did you take the money from my purse?

JOE: I just was going to borrow it. I would have put it back.

Turn to page 76 if you think this dialogue is correct.

_____C.

PARENT: Joe, where did you get that money?

JOE: From your purse.

PARENT: What is that called when you take without permission?

JOE: Stealing.

Turn to page 77 if you think this dialogue is correct.

page 74

If the child does not identify his behavior correctly or deliberately avoids identifying it because he knows what you want him to say, keep asking, "What else are you doing?" until he arrives at the correct response.

Once the child has identified his behavior, most parents will naturally tend to ask, "Why?" DON'T!! Don't ask for excuses. Remember, the child is responsible for his behavior. No matter how good a child's reasons are for doing an unacceptable act, the fact is that he still did the act and the reality of life is that he will experience the consequences of that act no matter how good his excuse for doing it. Therefore, don't invite excuses by asking "Why?" If excuses are volunteered, don't accept them as a justification for unacceptable behavior.

Which of the following dialogues illustrates correct handling of excuses?

_____A.
PARENT: What happened this morning when you went to school?
BETTE: I didn't make it on time.
PARENT: Is this the first time?
BETTE: No, I guess I've been late a lot this year. But I have to wait for Kathy at the corner so we can walk together. She's new in school this year and she doesn't have many friends. Some of the other girls are mean to her, so I walk with her to be friendly. She's late a lot, so I've been late a lot too.
PARENT: Oh Bette, I didn't know. That's very kind of you. But please, do the best you can to be on time from now on.

If you think this dialogue illustrates the correct handling of excuses, turn to page 79.

_____B.
PARENT: What happened this morning when you went to school?
BETTE: I didn't make it on time.
PARENT: Why didn't you?
BETTE: I had to wait for Kathy at the corner so we could walk together. She's new in school this year. Some of the other girls aren't nice to her, so I walk with her to be friendly. She's late a lot, so I've been late a lot.
PARENT: That's all very nice, Bette, but if you continue to be late to class you'll fall behind in your work and your teacher will be upset with you.

If you think this dialogue illustrates the correct handling of excuses, turn to page 80.

_____C.
PARENT: What happened this morning when you went to school?
BETTE: I didn't make it on time.
PARENT: Is this the first time?
BETTE: No, I guess I've been late a lot this year. But I have to wait for Kathy at the corner so we can walk together. She's new in school this year and she doesn't have many friends. Some of the other girls aren't nice to her, so I walk with her to be friendly. She's late a lot so I've been late a lot too.
PARENT: What happens when you keep coming to class late?
BETTE: I guess the teacher doesn't like it. She gets angry.
PARENT: What else?
BETTE: I miss some classwork and fall behind.

If you think this dialogue illustrates the correct handling of excuses, turn to page 81.

page 78

137

In which of the following dialogues is the child asked to make a value judgement of his act?

_____A.

JOHNNY: I was drawing on the wall.
PARENT: Is it right to draw on the wall?
JOHNNY: No, I guess not.

If this is correct, then turn to page 84.

_____B.

JOHNNY: I was drawing on the wall.
PARENT: Why were you doing that?
JOHNNY: Because I wanted to draw you a pretty picture. I looked for paper, but there wasn't any.

If this is correct, turn to page 85.

page 83

Which of the following dialogues leads the child to identify the consequences of his behavior?

_____A.

CHILD: I'm going to hit my crummy teacher. I hate her.
PARENT: What do you think will happen then?
CHILD: They'll probably throw me out of school.

If this is correct, turn to page 88.

_____B.

CHILD: I'm going to hit my crummy teacher. I hate her.
PARENT: I guess you know that you'll be kicked out of school.
CHILD: Yep. And I don't care.

If this is correct, turn to page 87.

page 86

In which of the following dialogues is the child helped to make a value judgement of the consequences of his behavior?

_____A.

PARENT: What happens when you steal?
CHILD: You have to go to juvenile court.
PARENT: Is that what you want?
CHILD: No.

Turn to page 91 if this is correct.

_____B.

PARENT: What do other people think of you when you steal?
MARY: They can't trust you.
PARENT: That's true, Mary, and I'm sure you don't want to become the type of person that cannot be trusted. What can you do to prevent this from happening?
MARY: I can stop taking things that don't belong to me.

Turn to page 90 if this is correct.

page 89

A
Short
Review

Once again, the four steps of RBT are:

1. Child identifies his behavior.
2. Child makes a value judgement of his behavior
                         and/or
3. Child identifies the consequences of his behavior and makes a value judgement of them.
4. Child formulates a plan and makes a commitment to follow it.

Let's see if you can use RBT now, referring only to the above summary of the process. Here is the situation:

Your family has a rule that nobody comes to breakfast before he washes his hands and face and combs his hair. Your daughter, Mary, comes to breakfast every day without first taking care of these details. You have to argue with her every morning before she will go back upstairs to wash and comb her hair. Today, as usual, Mary broke the family rule. What will your first statement or question to her be?

PARENT:

---

page 95

You should have led Mary to *identify her own behavior* (RBT Step One). For example, you could have asked, "What are you doing?" and Mary may have replied, "Getting ready to eat."

What would you say next?

PARENT:

page 96

Because Mary did not identify the behavior you were interested in talking about, you should have persevered in getting her to identify that behavior. You might have asked, "Have you missed doing anything this morning?" Actually, a simple "What else?" or "What kind of condition are you in?" would probably do the job. Then, Mary might reply, "I didn't get cleaned up."

We hope you recognize that you have two alternatives at this point and you can choose either one or both. If you choose to have Mary make a value judgement of her behavior, turn to page 98 as soon as you fill in your next response. If, on the other hand, you choose to have her identify the consequences of her behavior, turn to page 100 as soon as you fill in your next reply.

PARENT:

page 97

This is how your dialogue might have progressed: (We hope you didn't ask Mary for an excuse!)

PARENT: What are you doing?

MARY: Getting ready to eat.

PARENT: Have you forgotten to do anything this morning?

MARY: I didn't get cleaned up.

→ PARENT: Is it all right in our home to come to the table without washing your face and combing your hair?

MARY: No, but I don't see why we always have to wash first. It doesn't hurt anybody if we don't, does it?

PARENT:

Turn to the next page.

page 98

142

Your question/statement should lead Mary to identify a consequence of her action:

MARY: No, but I don't see why we always have to wash first. It doesn't hurt anybody if
          we don't, does it?

———▶ PARENT: (Pause for a moment and let the question clear.) What happens when you come
          downstairs and you are not cleaned up?

MARY: You throw a fit and yell at me.

PARENT:

Turn to the next page.

page 100

143

We hope you didn't let this answer throw you. Mary is trying to engage you in an argument. Don't be pulled off the track. Just keep the dialogue going until you get what you want.

> PARENT: What happens when you come downstairs and aren't cleaned up?
> MARY: You throw a fit and yell at me.
> → PARENT: What else?
> MARY: Well, I don't get to eat breakfast.
> PARENT:

page 101

You may have wanted to pursue other consequences, but since not getting breakfast is probably a consequence Mary does not want, you might ask her to make a value judgment of this consequence.

> CHILD: Well, I don't get to eat breakfast.
> PARENT: Is that what you want?
> CHILD: No.
> PARENT:

page 102

Once Mary evaluates the consequences of her behavior, you are ready to go on to the fourth step of RBT: formulation of a plan. Your next question should therefore lead the child to formulate a plan that will change her behavior.

          → PARENT: What are some of the things you can do to prevent your missing breakfast?

            CHILD: I could eat in my room where nobody would see me.

            PARENT: What else might you do?

            CHILD: I could try to get the rule changed.

            PARENT: You could. What else?

            CHILD: I could get up a little earlier so I could clean myself up in time for breakfast.

            PARENT: Yes, what else?

            CHILD: I can't think of anything else.

            PARENT:

page 103

There might have been some additional plans that Mary did not mention. But, she did come up with at least one good one, so you probably should have gone ahead and asked her to select one of the plans. (If she selects a plan that is completely objectionable to you, then let her know that the plan is not acceptable.) Your next statement/question should have been something like this:

MARY: I can't think of anything else.

→ PARENT: All right. Which of the plans do you think would be best for you?

MARY: I think I'll get up earlier.

PARENT: Good. Is there any way I can help?

MARY: Yes, I don't have an alarm clock and I think it would help a lot.

PARENT: I've got an extra one that your Dad uses on trips. You can have it.

MARY: Thanks, Mom.

PARENT:

page 104

Post-Test

The following test is identical to the pretest you took at the beginning of Lesson III. After you have finished, score both your pre- and post-tests using the key on page 110. Compare your tests. What did you learn? Did any of your ideas or opinions change?

1. Children should always be allowed to find their own solutions to their problems.   T   F

2. If my child says he will do something, I do not have to follow up to be sure he did it.   T   F

3. If I checked up on my child, I would feel that I was not trusting him.   T   F

4. My teen-ager knows what will happen to him if he does something wrong.   T   F

5. There is nothing wrong with the following exchange:
   FATHER: You know what you did was wrong, don't you?
   CHILD: Yes.   T   F

6. It is a good idea always to ask your child to explain why he did what he did.   T   F

7. If your child fails to change his behavior after a number of attempts, it is usually because he does not want to change.   T   F

8. Every child wants to love and be loved, no matter how disobedient or mean.   T   F

9. A positive relationship is not essential to teaching your child responsible behavior.   T   F

10. The best time to solve a child's behavior problem is as soon as it is noticeable.   T   F

page 109

Notes